TAKING BACK THE COURTS

What We Can Do
To Reclaim Our Sovereignty

SUTTON HART PRESS

TAKING BACK THE COURTS

What We Can Do
To Reclaim Our Sovereignty

NORM PATTIS

FOREWORD BY F. LEE BAILEY
INTRODUCTION BY GERRY SPENCE

SUTTON HART PRESS

Taking Back the Courts is published by Sutton Hart Press LLC

P.O. 5647 Vancouver, Washington 98668

Inquiries: information@suttonhart.com

Website: www.suttonhart.com

First printing August, 2011

ISBN: 978-0-9819888-5-6

LCCN: 2011927519

Library of Congress Cataloging-In-Publication Data Has Been Applied For

Printed in the United States of America

Media & Reviewer Contact: maggie@platformstrategy.com

Cover design: Maria Elias and Jason Enterline

Copy editor: Julie Fusella

Layout design: Jason Enterline

Cover image: Getty Images

Dedication

To Judy, who is everything to me and to Oscar Hills, a tutor in courage.

CONTENTS

FOREWORD

BY F. LEE BAILEY

Several years ago I was asked by my most important client at the time to find him a fearless, highly skilled lawyer in Connecticut to take the lead in a monstrous case which was then degenerating rapidly. After questioning a number of colleagues to get recommendations, I set an interview with Norman Pattis of New Haven. We met at dinner. At first glance, as he entered the room, I noted a generous pony-tail, patches on the elbows of his sport coat, a shirt suitable for fly-fishing, and a pair of shoes that must have come from L. L. Bean. This was how he dressed for court. In my mind I imposed on him an indictment for "hippiness", and envisioned great problems in getting my client - who had many of the attributes of a tiger - to even agree to an introduction. Thirty minutes later, the indictment dissolved, I stepped out of the room and called the client: "I have our guy," I said. "Good," said the client. "Sign him up!" Thus began an always intriguing and consistently pleasant relationship which has lasted since that day and has, I hope, a long future; I have invited Norm to my 100th birthday party.

We worked together on the monster litigation, and got what I consider to be a good result. Not long after it was concluded, I asked him to handle a tragic case for a friend, wherein a young mother was charged with vehicular manslaughter and driving under the influence of alcohol resulting from a crash which killed two of her children, and nearly killed her. He took the case to trial (as described in the book) and turned in a masterful job.

Norman has an exquisite command of the written word, and his prose in this book soars and swoops consistently. For those whose English skills are less than extraordinary, the book is worth reading regardless of its content, just to get the benefit of writing at its best. I have written several million words myself, and always felt that I had a pretty good handle on the King's English. Pattis sent me to the dictionary six times in less than 200 pages, read carefully in just over five hours on a Sunday. Most of these trips were worthwhile, although Pattis flirts with the pedantic when he uses "quotidian", when "mundane" will work just as well or better.

It is said that a lawyer who will represent the poor, the downtrodden, the hated and the ugly, against the juggernaut of the state, must have balls of a lion. Having tried my first case in 1954, and having tracked the very best trial lawyers since that time so I could learn from them, I must endorse the description above. But such a lawyer must also have the unflagging stamina of a marathon runner, the calm under fire of a David who has but one chance to bring down Goliath, and a simmering rage against the law and its minions that often lumber along almost mindlessly, crushing the good with the evil. Such a warrior must also have the most rare among the skills of an advocate: a consummate command of the spoken word. Pattis stands very, very tall in this respect. He is one of the best speakers I have ever encountered.

He has the arsenal which best befits a gunslinger: a Colt .44, a 30-30 deer rifle and a Bowie knife. These are all in the form of whiplash phrases and sentences so necessary to the destruction of a lying witness, with which our courtrooms are well-populated.

This is not to say that Norman Pattis is perfect. His massive indictment of all judges and prosecutors as ranging from lazy and meek to the devil incarnate is overdone. As one who has had a handle in some form in court cases in every state of the United States but Montana, I have found most of our judges to be pretty good; they would be better if we paid them a realistic wage. True, several of them were ugly and cruel people inside and out, and should be publicly defrocked and thrown bodily off the bench. And while too many prosecutors take unto themselves a license to massage the truth in order to win the case, I have met a goodly number who had some sense of "doing the right thing".

Pattis is seriously wrong-headed with nearly all of what he has to say about the Simpson case - but I will fix that. He makes good inroads into some of the things that are wrongfully done to minimal sex-offenders, but doesn't complete the circle. True pedophiles need some sorts of controls, because their lust can and often does degenerate into murder and rape (in that order). On the other hand, awarding the next slot on the U. S. Supreme Court to a trial lawyer who has lived in the pit and on the street is a very good idea: President Obama and Attorney General Holder, please take note.

This is an important book. For all who contemplate or are engaged in the study of law, it should be required reading. Even those students who plan to hide out in the comfort of the nooks and garrets of some behemoth law firm, insulated from the hurly-burly of our courts, need a solid glimpse of what really goes on before they write their briefs whose purpose is to crush some "little guy" opponent. It is essential for these "quiet ones" to realize that the Pattis type is a vanishing breed, slowly being crushed by courts at the behest of prosecutors who have been given way too much power by lawmakers. There are no other real hotshots, to my knowledge, coming down the pike. Not for many, many years has a top-ranked trial lawyer, possessed of a superb vocabulary, ripped open the innards of a system which has multitudinous shortcomings and a goodly number of sins festering in its underbelly. Judges who are offended, and prosecutors and police who are outraged, may seek revenge. They should be careful. This horse can kick and bite.

Among those of us who have sallied forth into the breach of the well of the court, broadsword and scimitar firmly in hand, the litmus test for the really top-shelf lawyers who occupy these halls is simply this: If I were in some sort of serious trouble, who would I choose? Who would I trust to give me the very best representation, shrewdly and fearlessly. This is where the rubber meets the road.

I have long maintained such a list. It is rather short now, since a number of my esteemed colleagues who did *not* resolve to live to be 100 have passed along in recent years. But the list, however brief, remains. The youngest, but by no means the least, of the names on that list is Norman Pattis.

F. Lee Bailey

INTRODUCTION

BY GERRY SPENCE

To understand the nefarious carryings-on of the justice system you must ignore as irrelevant the professors who peddle to unwary law students and to the lobotomized bar ideas that are as archaic as the medical profession's leaches of old. You must uniformly disbelieve as naked fraud the promises of politicians who holler and rot as they swim in their own political excrement. You must irreverently question the pronouncements of judges who pound their judicial breasts like drummers on soggy drums and demand the nation to dance to their doleful tunes, and finally you must read this book written by a man who knows the justice system, because he has not only lived in it for many years but examined it, absorbed it, tested it, peered at it like a pathologist examining a diseased spleen, confronted it, challenged it to be real and honest, a man who has refused to accept its mythology, who has been disappointed by the system, amazed at its deficiencies, disgusted by its lack of human compassion, confounded at its hypocrisy, amused by it folly and disappointed by its failure to respond to live people instead of dead money.

Pattis is one of the best, a genuine trial lawyer, who has labored and wept and hoped and skillfully fought just battles in these temples where justice is said to reside, and who, over these pages, reports his findings on certain questions: Is this system even marginally adequate to protect the revered rights of a free people? Is it sufficient to admit it has faults, but with a shrug, acknowledge it is a human institution and, as such, it will suffer its own pathology? At last, is it permissible to offer one's lips to that worn out aphorism holding that, despite its faults, it is the best system in the world, and thereby, having made our confession of its deficiencies, to bounce blithely and blindly along, decade after decade, with a judiciary that has betrayed the people's trust? So is the justice system in this country broken?

Well, yes.

Do we care?

We are lied to so thoroughly and skillfully that we don't appreciate how sick the system is until we must face it ourselves, until we look for the few lawyers and judges who understand it and who, if they understand it, care enough or are brave enough to expose it. We must not undress it, for if we do we may be approaching heresy considering the system's demand that we be ever reverential in its face – sort of like the maxim that forbids publically condemning at his funeral the villainous dead lying in his open coffin. Lawyers are taught they must respect judges some of whom are not entitled to respect, even as members of the species. Lawyers are charged with the duty to bow courteously to an opponent no matter that he is a retched cur and a blight on the profession. Lawyers are required to respect the institution of the court despite that in the hands of unfettered and ignorant power it produces pain and injustice that would occasion any honest person to rise up in loathing and horror.

I am reasonably fond of the polemic I have just written. But I like the facts and the examples, the elegant prose, the tough and intelligent insights and stories of Mr. Pattis better. We yearn for someone to tell us the truth. Please do not lie to me any more. Please do not defraud me again. Please do not promise me justice when, in most cases, it is available only for those with money. Please do not turn untrained lawyers loose in the courtrooms to fight for the accused, public defenders, who have a hundred cases and who are given neither the time nor the facilities to prepare for even one, and who are forced to join in the nauseating games being played in every jurisdiction in America where clients are pled guilty to crimes they did not commit or who possess valid defenses against the charges—all of which is performed in the name of due process but proves to be little more than the nation's barefaced lie proclaiming, without embarrassment, that there is liberty and justice for all.

Mr. Pattis does not write with such dripping vehemence. He is far too able and gracious to do so. But what he writes in well-balanced, well nourished prose is true. The courts belong to us. They are not the property of judges many of whom sit on high because they suffer a latent and virulent lust for judging others. The courts are not the property of mediocre lawyers, now judges, who could not otherwise make a go of the devilish demands of a private practice. The courts do not belong to the politicians who infect our hoped-for wholesomeness of the judiciary with the pernicious political agendas of those who appoint them to these scared posts. The courts belong to the people. The function of our courts is to keep presidents and congressmen and corporations contaminated with greed for money and power from destroying our dreams of a more fulfilling life and from denying justice over the broken rights and bodies of the people. The courts are diseased. Justice has become an empty word. The people see themselves as helpless. Pattis tells us we must take the courts back. He proves his case herein.

xvi • *Norm Pattis*

And, now what? Well, let me say it: It got this way because of you. It will remain in this devilish condition as long as you are willing to endure it. When you finish this book you will have been put on what the law calls "inquiry notice." You will have been fully advised, enough so that you must inquire further. The condition Pattis describes will become terminal if you do nothing, and all the while we will hear the same blaring rhetoric about the beauty of our court system. But you ought not care. The system only fails those who do not have the means. At least it fails only those who come before it seeking the promise of justice or who are dragged before it in cuffs and chains. That will not be you, of course. Not ever. That will not be your child or loved one.

No. Not ever.

Gerry Spence

PREFACE

Government amazes me; the state terrifies. Try as I might, the sense of it all eludes me. We might not have been born free, but the chains we routinely accept are heavy weights. I rage against them blindly and without real hope of lasting victory. I rage against them because I am not prepared to die a servant of strangers. I rage against them and am therefore a trial lawyer. I defend people against the monsters we create.

The German philosopher Immanuel Kant once wrote that two things filled him with awe: the starry heavens above, and the moral law within. Let me add a third source of wonder: the fact that perfect strangers acquire not just power, but the right, to tell others how to live. This third miracle is government. It is a miracle that can be used for good or ill.

How good is American government? Oh, I know the platitudes. We are the land of the free. We are a city on a hill. We are a beacon to the world. Why, everything is just fine and dandy. God Bless America, we sing. And we mean it, too, at least most of the time.

But I wonder how many of us really enjoy the liberty we proclaim on the Fourth of July? When I read about a man and his family being evicted from their home because they can't pay their mortgage, freedom rings a little hollow. When I hear about high unemployment, lack of health care, schools that fail, and then I read about corporate bailouts and the lifestyles of the rich and famous, I can't help but wonder whether there are at least two Americas. There is the daylight dream realized by the elite, and then there is the waking nightmare of the great mass of folks struggling in quiet desperation. Where, I wonder, do these two worlds even meet? Do they ever meet?

The polling place is one place where Americans have a voice. But it is not much of a voice. Although Barack Obama mobilized a lot of new voters and promised change, the landscape doesn't look much different a couple of years after his election. The rich are getting richer; the poor remain poor; and the same old elites are in charge of the courts, our corporations and our public institutions. Plenty of folks are looking for more radical change. They are looking for hope. They are looking for justice, whether that be social justice, criminal justice, civil justice, or economic justice.

We are a court-watching people. Turn the television on in the evening and the screen glows with images of police officers solving crimes. Courtroom dramas are the stuff of daily news. Tongues wag about the doings in our courts. Why are we so preoccupied with the courts?

We are transfixed because we believe that it is in a courtroom that we can be heard. We expect juries to be composed of people just like us. It is in a jury trial that we expect the miracle of government to be made plain and transparent to all Americans. If each of us can serve on a jury, if each of us truly has access to a courtroom, then each of us can redeem the promise of American life by seeking justice. The courts are the engine of democracy, the ancient Athenian forum brought to life in twenty-first century form. At least that is my vision of what the courts should be.

The sad reality is that what goes on in a courtroom is a long way from fulfilling the dream of civic participation in the broadest and most significant issues of the day. The courts are drifting out of control. Lawyers and judges, armed with an arcane vocabulary and near magical powers, can summon us into a courtroom and then make a mockery of our dreams for autonomy and civic responsibility. The courts are out of control, and unless we take them back, this most accessible form of self-government and regulation of government conduct will become a closed and cloistered world, as far removed from the lives of ordinary Americans as the doings in a corporate boardroom or the shenanigans in a Senator's suite on Capitol Hill.

There's time to take back the courts, but just barely. If we want to regain control of how justice is administered and of the shape of our day to day lives, whether it be whom we love, how we live, where we work, and to whom we are accountable, we must act now. Things are far worse than the rhetoric we use to describe our lives acknowledges. If you want to provoke change, you must demand answers and insist on transparency.

I am a trial lawyer. I go to court almost every day and fight for people. Most of my cases involve a fight with the government. Either a client has been charged with a crime and has hired me to fight for his life and liberty, or, in some cases, I pick the fight with a government employee, filing a civil suit on behalf of an ordinary man or woman who believes that the government has abused them. I have issues with authority. Sometimes I represent individuals in private disputes; these affairs are usually tense and difficult. A man may be fighting to see his children, or someone might sue the woman who falsely accused him of exposing himself to her child.

I am a warrior and I am bold enough to assert here that I fight as well as any lawyer alive. When I pick up a newspaper in the morning and learn of a new conflict or controversy, some part of me always wishes that I had the case in question. Why would someone go elsewhere, I wonder? It says a lot about my ego, I suppose, that I genuinely believe this. As I worked on this book, Julian Assange, identified as the founder of WikiLeaks, was taken into custody in Great Britain. All at once, I was filled with longing to represent him. I suppose I am lucky; I have found my place in the world. I am on David's side in every fight; there are Goliaths everywhere in need of slaying. I have a pocket full of stones and a sharp aim. I love the feeling when the giant stumbles and falls. The blood of tyrants nurtures liberty.

I make no apologies for my role or attitude. I've made my share of friends, and more than my share of enemies. But that is as it should be with a life well lived. A group of people marching lockstep is quickly hypnotized by the cadence of uniformity. A government unchallenged by those it governs becomes arrogant and haughty. Whether we are the product of creation or evolution, I am inspired by the thought that we are all equal and that no person is the sum of his worst moments. I am the last friend of the friendless, a warrior for the despised, a thorn in the side of the popular and powerful. I am hated until I am needed, and then I am the last hope of the hopeless. I am, I repeat again, a trial lawyer, and I intend to die one, hopefully in a courtroom, breathing my last bits of fire into the cold face of an autocrat.

This book is a series of snapshots of things I have seen in court. These sketches of cases, controversies and events won't find their way onto a scholar's shelf. Don't expect a design for a better world. Power often justifies itself by saying to the critic: "I am necessary. Design a better system or forfeit the right to speak." Says who? Sometimes it is enough to speak. I don't recall Jesus of Nazareth penning any great manifestos about a better government before he was nailed to a cross. It was enough for him to proclaim that the Kingdom of God was at hand: this both got him killed and kept us scratching our heads now for two thousand years. It is enough, I tell you, to look the Devil in the eye and demand simply that he blink.

Some of the material in this book first appeared in the form of columns printed in the Connecticut Law Tribune, for which I have written a weekly column for the past decade. I've changed some of these columns somewhat, trying to eliminate what are now anachronisms, and from time to time correcting errors of fact or omission that I made in the mad scramble to write a weekly column. A special thanks to the good folks at American Lawyers Media for permission to use the material here. Other portions of this book have appeared on various blog pages I have written for the past five years. I try to write something daily at www.pattisblog.com, but some days I am simply too swamped to opine. A busy law practice can do that do to even the most opinionated man. I've changed most of the names of former clients in this book, unless their case has already received so much attention as to cross the threshold from routine to notorious. And I've disclosed no confidences here. I may from time to time engage in poetic license to reflect a client's position or how the client was perceived. Those looking to find fault with this technique can have the satisfaction of doing so. I learned long ago that peck sniffs are a constant in this life. Sniff away.

"More light, less heat," a judge once told me as I argued heart and soul in favor of just what I can't recall. The judge won't like this book: it is heat; the fire that burns my clients more often than not in places where light should shine. Consider this book a quick diagnostic tour of our palaces of justice. Most of you don't visit courtrooms daily. I do. This is what I see and, I am telling you, the courts are failing. Read this, look for yourself, then together let's find a better way to do justice.

The book is intended to comfort the afflicted and to afflict the comfortable. It is an invitation to walk in the shadow of darkness and death, only to find the courage that comes of honest despair. I invite you to travel along, and to look for your own pebble or stone to throw against the glass towers of the high and mighty. Come walk with me down a rebel's lane. The journey, however short or long it may be, begins not with a single step, but with the turning of this page ...

CHAPTER 1

WHERE ARE WE?

Perhaps you've lost your job, or maybe your home is in foreclosure. Maybe you're one of the lucky few who made it through tough economic times more or less in one piece. You might even be a banker who mortgaged the nation's future in a fraud, failed, and then got a government-backed bailout. Whoever you are, odds are you sit up from time to time and wonder whether the rhetoric of the American dream really and truly matches the reality of your life. Did "we the people" really bargain for what amounts to chaos? Many, if not most, Americans feel as though the American dream has been betrayed. Some seek to reclaim it through religion, others through political firestorms, and others still have opted out entirely, content to find what stability and comfort they can in the security of private associations.

But there is still one place where we the people can speak loudly and clearly. That is in a courtroom. Criminal cases and many civil cases are decided daily in the courts by ordinary Americans sitting on juries. The jury system is at risk, however. We are emasculating the jury system with lies, legal doctrines and biases that are making trials less a chance for the people to decide cases and controversies than a privileged arena for judges and the well-heeled to decide what justice requires in ever broader areas of American life. I say it's time to take back the courtrooms, one jury at a time. Doing so requires a little planning and insight into what goes on in a courtroom, so I am offering this small book, based largely on my own experiences in the past couple of decades, as a tool you can use to reclaim a sense of power.

Consider the following: what would you do if you were standing at a street corner waiting for the light to change, and two young men walked up to you, pulled a gun and ordered you to produce your wallet? I suspect most of us would comply. We would give up our wallet, although not our sense of outrage, out of a sense of self-preservation. The armed men have the power to compel us to do their will. We may not know the men at all, but force speaks.

But suppose these two young men were wearing the uniforms of our local police department? We see on their shoulder a patch naming the department. They have a nameplate above their breast pocket announcing their last name. They appear to be clean cut and reasonably well-spoken.

Although we would still be alarmed and unhappy to be looking down the barrel of their guns, we would comply with the command to produce our wallet. At some level, we would accept that these men had not just the power to compel us to do their will, but also that the police officers had the right to compel us to act.

In the case of the two young men at the street corner, we comply with their show of force because they have the apparent power to cause us harm. We comply with the police for similar reasons, but there is more to their show of force: we acknowledge their authority to use force. The difference between mere power and authority is a sense of legitimacy. We say of the state that it has a monopoly on the legitimate use of force.

But we say far more than that in the United States. We say that authority is exercised in our name, in the name of We the People. The Preamble to the federal Constitution begins with those words. Our Bill of Rights guarantees us rights that the government is not supposed to be able to trample upon. These rights are not self-enforcing, however. If they are to mean anything at all, we the people must have a place where we can go to make government listen, and to hold government accountable. It's not enough to vote every couple of years, especially if all the men and women running for office start to look and sound the same. We the people need a place to turn to be heard in the day-to-day matters of importance to us in our communities. I say that the courts can be and should be such a place.

In a healthy republic, we would say that the police officer acted in our name when he pulled a gun to stop and question someone. We have authorized his action in a way we never would the drug lords. But my sense is that we are a long way from healthy as a society. We have permitted police officers to become as unaccountable as the giant corporations they protect. When a banker comes to take our home on behalf of an investor betting against our success, the banker is often accompanied by a police officer. Who authorized this turning of our guns against ourselves? I did not. Did you?

Ordinary Americans should be able to turn to the courts for relief. We should be able to make our case for justice in front of an ordinary jury of our peers. We ought to be able to say to the corporation that fouling our waters creates an obligation to clean them, that being too big to fail means that you must ensure we succeed. We ought to be able to say to a police officer that using high voltage to prod us like cattle from one spot to another is wrong. Juries should be able to say to judge, prosecutor and lawmaker that some laws don't make sense.

But the courts are out of control and adrift just now. Judges have assumed powers in the name of the people that we have never given them. Jurors are lied to and misled. Lawmakers refuse to be accountable for the consequences of what they do in the courts. Lawyers grow fat, sassy and increasingly disengaged from the pursuit of justice. Whether in civil or criminal court, the pursuit of justice looks more and more like a game played by hidden rules. All this and more is done in the name of you the people. What do you say we do something about it, you and I?

The first step in reclaiming the courts is understanding that a courtroom is a place of public terror. It is where strangers face one another in contests that often determine what becomes of them and their fortunes. The courtroom is the place in our society where we try to transform naked power into authority. Force is applied in a courtroom, and that force is supposed to be the people's force, force applied in your name. If you are unhappy with what you see taking place in the courtrooms of this nation, you should be as outraged as you would be if you saw your church desecrated or your home invaded by strangers.

Most of our ideas about justice and public life come from Greece and Rome. The Roman orator Cicero once wrote that a republic is not just any collection of human beings united together; a republic is a group of people bound together by common interests and a shared conception of right, or justice. In the United States, we claim the Constitution is the document reflecting our shared sense of right. The Constitution is not a mere contract binding strangers together in a common enterprise. Rather, the Constitution is a shared commitment creating a community.

But who decides what the Constitution says or what it means? What role do the people have in defining and redefining common visions uniting strangers under law? Did we the people really rebel against a distant overlord, declare our independence, create a new Constitution and then decide to walk away from that creation, leaving it in the hands of others to interpret?

We certainly behave that way. Would anyone today really protest over a tax on tea or coffee? I'm not talking about the polite sort of water cooler protesting that takes place at work. I'm talking about the sort of protest that inspired men to dump tea into Boston Harbor in defiance of British power.

I am not suggesting that a social revolution will solve the problems confronting us. The twentieth century was among the most violent centuries in history because one utopian vision after another was set loose on ordinary people in the name of the good. In each case, the utopia became a living hell. It did so because of what I call the Rule of the Eleventh Man. It works something like this.

Put a group of ten people together in a room for a while. Leave them alone. Soon enough, a group will form, with a common sense of identity and some sense of pecking order. In no time at all, they will come to think of themselves as sharing something, even if they cannot name what it is that is shared.

Now, let an eleventh man walk in after this group has taken shape. Try as he might, the eleventh man will not quite fit in. The group has now become large enough, complex enough, that there are insiders and outsiders. To protect what they have in common, the group will turn on the eleventh man. He is the outcast, the heretic. He'll be ostracized, perhaps locked away or even killed, depending on the stakes. Every utopia becomes a living hell to the outsider. The last thing we need is another utopia.

The courts can serve as a means of leveling the playing field between insider and outsider in all spheres of life. But to do that, jurors and citizens appearing in the courtrooms of this nation need to do less bowing and scraping before a judge. Every time I see a court open session and hear a marshal command all to rise as the judge enters the room, some part of me dies. How has it come to pass that in a republic we treat judges like kings? What sorts of pompous asses require we the people to refer to them as "your honor"? Judges ought to stand as we the people enter the room; they serve the community.

So here is the first thing you can do to recapture the courts: stop pretending that judges are divine or semi-divine oracles dispensing wisdom from the bench. They put their shoes on the same way you do; they only choose to dress funny to create a sense of distance between themselves and all others in the courtroom. A judge is entitled to decent respect, to be sure; but no more respect than is due the man or woman accused of a crime, or seeking compensation for an injury. We have no priestly caste from which judges are drawn. Anyone can become a judge in this country. You can become a judge. In fact, you are a judge of what goes on in our courtrooms. I wonder what would happen if you went to a courtroom just to watch the proceedings, to let the judge know that the people are present. Instead of standing as the judge enters, remain seated. When the marshal orders you to stand, ask him, "Why? What law requires this?" He will not be able to recite such a law because there is none. But odds are he will ask you to leave the court. Indeed, the judge may order you to do so. Why, again? You have a First Amendment right to attend court proceedings; no legal duty requires you to stand when the judge enters. I predict that if this small symbolic step were to take place in courtrooms throughout the country day by day, it would be as symbolic a gesture as dumping tea in Boston Harbor. Do you care enough about your liberty to take this small step?

What good does all this do? Aren't there bigger issues, such as racial justice, insane drug laws, corporations that avoid accountability, the rape of the Earth? How will these little steps change anything? In and of themselves, these steps change nothing. But what they signify is a change in attitude, and that is where revolutionary change begins.

There's no use pretending that when the colonists arrived on the shores of North America, they arrived on an empty continent with divine blessing to build a city on a hill for all the world to admire. There were native Americans here. Many of them died when exposed to diseases brought to these shores from Europe. Others were killed fighting to protect a way of life threatened by an invading people. There was no state of nature extant on our shores, no blank slate on which men and women could confront one another without the restraining influence of law and then decide what rules would best govern their affairs. Yet theories about the state of nature and the formation of civil society are powerful means of explaining how authority is distributed and what justice requires. So let's pretend, shall we, that we live in a state of nature; there is no government to protect us from one another. It's a jungle out there. The strong consume the weak. That doesn't sound like a fantasy? It sounds real? That's all the more reason to press on.

I want to end this chapter where I began it. What makes a cop different than a gangbanger when you are looking down the barrel of a stranger's gun? The difference is that the police officer's show of force is legitimate because he is said to be acting with authority, he is said to be acting in our name. The gangbanger, by contrast, demonstrates mere power; his use of force reflects a private purpose we do not share.

Social contract theory explains how a government acquires legitimacy. In the absence of any government, people are said to live in a state of nature. To acquire security and the means to accomplish other common purposes, people in the state of nature give up natural liberty in exchange for the security provided by the state. The social contract they form authorizes the state to act on behalf of all of them to establish common norms and to enforce these norms with force if necessary. What is important about this contract is that it makes legitimacy flow from consent of the governed. Consent is the basis of authority in a democratic society.

Tell me, did you consent to the decision to bail out Wall Street tycoons while ordinary Americans lost their homes to foreclosure? I sure as hell did not. My congresswoman voted in favor of doing this, but she didn't ask me. I'm supposed to sit tight and bide my time until the next election to signify my approval or disapproval of this Welfare for Wall Street scam. From where I sit, however, the bailouts look a lot like behavior in the state of nature. Rich bankers get their powerful friends to screw little people without either power or wealth. It is enough to make me want to holler.

I propose the following test to evaluate a policy measure or law. If I were on the short end of the law's stick, would I think the law fair? If so, then the law is just; if not, the law is not fair. I'm not the person who first conceived this theory. John Rawls, a Harvard professor, did so almost fifty years ago in an essay called "Justice as Fairness." He devoted a long academic career to defending the idea, eventually defending it in his longer book, *A Theory of Justice.*

Let's use this notion of justice as fairness as the touchstone for the following analysis of our courts and legal system. I encourage you to adopt the standpoint of a person in the state of nature. You know only the general shape and structure of our society: you know there are people of color, bankers, athletes, judges, single mothers. But in the state of nature you just don't know what role you will be assigned in society. Will you be lucky, and be an athlete of incredible skill and grace? Or will you be unlucky, and find yourself mentally ill, without family and friends to support you? How fair is life when seen from the bottom of the heap?

I've been going to court almost every day for almost 20 years, representing people on the short end of the stick. I once represented a prisoner beaten by guards in a failed escape attempt. I once represented a frail old woman who was roughed up by police officers as she watched them arrest her son in her own home. I have represented men merely present when bad acts occurred but charged now as coconspirators in crimes that require they be locked away for a lifetime. I've learned up close and personal the extent to which power will go to protect its own. I've learned that for little people, justice isn't fairness. Clarence Darrow perhaps got it right: there is no such thing as justice inside or out of court.

But I cannot give up longing for justice. Neither, I suspect, can you. You want a way to fight back against what sickens you. It's not enough to sit back and wait for the next election cycle when you will be given the meaningless choice between Tweedledee and Tweddledum as candidates for high office. We live our lives in the here and now. We want ways to affect the world around us today, not two years from today, assuming the next candidate for whom we vote has the courage of whatever convictions our politics make it safe for him to utter.

My hunch is that increasing numbers of Americans look at what goes on in a courtroom the way strangers might view gangbanging men with guns: strangers, making up rules as they go along, extracting things from others with power and fear. We are becoming strangers in our own courts. I say it's time we take them back.

I want to tell you what I see in the courts. I want to tell you what I see and ask for your help making it better. I believe the courts belong to the people but that judges, prosecutors and defense lawyers are taking the courts away, bit by bit. What follows are observations in no particular order. These are things that I have seen; things that happened and continue to happen in your name. Do you care enough to demand change?

CHAPTER 2

WHO IS THE
SOVEREIGN AFTER ALL?

I recall well what I was doing the morning jets slammed into the World Trade Center. It was a bright day in New England, a crisp, sunny sort of September day that held the energetic promise of fall, my favorite season. My phone rang. Had I heard about the accident in New York? A plane had flown into one of the World Trade Center buildings. I assumed it was an accident, and did not give it much thought. But then the telephone rang again; another plane had flown into the second building. We turned on a television in my law firm's lunchroom and watched the smoke pour out of the buildings. These were no accidents. This was terror. In the course of a few hours, it was obvious that this was a dangerous time to be an American, perhaps as dangerous a time as any since President Abraham Lincoln suspended the writ of habeas corpus during the civil war, making it impossible for those seized unlawfully by government to seek their freedom in courts.

I was not so much frightened by the prospect of another plane slamming into a building, a luxury I suppose I could afford living as I did in a small town without any extraordinary targets. What I worried about was how the government, the courts, and we the people would react to the terrorist attacks. We get the government we deserve, and it struck me that day, as it strikes me now, that the Fourth Amendment was the real target of the terrorists. Because they could not attack the

Constitution itself, they attacked our peace of mind. They left it to us to destroy our own Constitution.

The federal Constitution is little read, and even less understood. When is the last time you actually read the Constitution? Odds are it has been a long time, if ever at all. But the Constitution defines in the broadest possible terms who we are as a people. It is the contested terrain of our moral and cultural life. The Constitution limits the power of government; it draws lines beyond which the government cannot go. One set of those lines is the Fourth Amendment guarantee we enjoy against unreasonable searches and seizures. It is the source of such things as the requirement that the police have a warrant signed by a neutral and detached magistrate before they search your home.

But here's the rub. The Constitution doesn't define what reasonable means. The definition of what is and is not reasonable is left to the courts. Judges decide what is and is not reasonable, and their decisions become binding law. And judges decide what is and is not reasonable, much like umpires behind home plate decide the contours of a strike zone.

One of the leading United States Supreme Court decisions on how to interpret the Fourth Amendment holds that the government's power to search will be deemed unreasonable only if the government seeks to search an area in which a person has an expectation of privacy that the community at large is prepared to regard as justified. In that case, decided at a time before cell phones, when pay phones stood in enclosed phone booths, the Court held that police officers could attach a device to the outside of a telephone booth to listen to the conversations of someone using the phone. Sure, the speaker might expect that his conversation was private, but, the Court concluded, the rest of us did not think this belief was reasonable. The result was the Fourth Amendment did not prohibit the government from eavesdropping on conversations arising from telephone booth conversations.

This decision has always troubled me. The Constitution suddenly seems less like a stalwart guardian of an individual's right to be let alone, than an exercise in group therapy, with nine Supreme Court justices playing the role of therapists. Just how are justices supposed to decide what the nation regards as reasonable?

In the days following the 9/11 attacks, it seemed obvious to me that many Americans were prepared to sacrifice plenty of liberty for a sense of security. The greatest threat to our freedom from unlawful search and seizure is not the government, it is our fear. Will we too easily trade liberty for a false sense of security?

In the decade that followed the World Trade Center catastrophe, the nation's courts have retreated from any meaningful role in protecting a robust sense of liberty. We have let them do it without so much as a whimper. There has been a silent revolution by judicial activists posturing as jurists concerned with keeping judges from wielding too much power. Their weapon of choice has been a doctrine called qualified immunity. This judicially created fiction has slammed shut the nation's courthouse doors to ordinary people seeking to hold government actors accountable. This most silent of revolutions is the work of lifetime appointees to the federal bench. We the people were never consulted.

In the wake of the Civil War, Congress passed legislation known as the Ku Klux Klan Act. This law gave ordinary people the right to sue government employees if those employees violated a person's legal rights. The act was intended to provide access to justice to persons of color or others unable to enjoy the law's full measure of protection in communities in which local and state government was uncommitted to equal justice for all.

The act went largely unused for many years until the 1960s. After Chicago police officers burst into the home of a black man and terrorized his family while questioning him about a murder, the man sued the police, claiming they had violated his rights to be free from unreasonable searches and seizures. The police officers tried to get the suit thrown out of court, claiming that they were immune from suit since they were, in effect, state actors. They claimed the benefit of something called sovereign immunity.

You can read the Constitution one hundred and fifty times, until your eyes fall out, until the paper on which it is printed disintegrates. Read it as many times as you like and you will never see the words sovereign immunity. Yet the courts apply this doctrine daily to make state officials immune from justice. It is an ancient legal doctrine applicable to kings and emperors; it has no place in a republic. The courts use the doctrine daily to keep the people from bringing legal claims against the government and its employees in court. Erwin Chemerinsky, one of the nation's top Constitutional law scholars, is dead right when he observes, in his new book, *The Conservative Assault on the Constitution*:

"A doctrine derived from the premise 'the king can do no wrong' deserves no place in American law. The United States was founded on rejection of monarchy and royal prerogative. American government is based on the fundamental recognition that the government and government officials can do wrong and must be held accountable. Sovereign immunity undermines that basic notion."

In the Chicago case, the Supreme Court engaged in some creative reasoning. It concluded that although the police officers were on the job when they burst into the plaintiff's home, they were not shielded by sovereign immunity in their capacity as individuals. They could be sued for violating the law they had sworn a duty to uphold. But the City of Chicago could not be sued for the unlawful acts of the officers. Such are the distinctions the law draws; keeping track of them is the monopoly of lawyers. We incant these doctrines much like priests conjuring the assistance of gods and goddesses.

The courts exploded with lawsuits challenging official misconduct after the Chicago case. I myself have been involved in hundreds of lawsuits challenging the authority of a police officer to arrest a person, to search a person's home or car, to use force against a person during an arrest. These are all civil actions, and a plaintiff who prevails in them is entitled not just to an award of money damages for the loss of their rights. The law permits a jury, acting as the conscience of the community, to make an award of punitive damages as well. Punitive damages are intended to deter similar misconduct by others and to punish a person who violated a person's rights.

During the past decade, judges have been very busy slamming the doors to the courthouse shut on these claims. They are doing so not because Congress asked them to, or because the Constitution requires it. They are doing it as part of a silent revolution that few seem to notice. The legal vehicle by which they are doing this is a doctrine most Americans have never heard of. Not content with mere sovereign immunity, judges have drummed up a new outrage, a legal doctrine called qualified immunity. These immunities make it almost impossible for an ordinary person to get justice when a public official abuses them.

How did this happen? Why are we letting this occur?

Immunities aren't all that difficult a concept to grasp. If the law is a vast set of rules defining what we can and cannot accomplish in a court of law, an immunity is simply a device by which a judge declares a person off limits. Suppose, for example, that your neighbor stands on the corner and shouts for all the world to hear that you are a terrorist. This harm to your reputation might well give rise to a lawsuit by you against your neighbor claiming defamation of character. It is, after all, damaging to your reputation to be labeled a terrorist.

But suppose a lawmaker were to assert a similar claim during debate on the floor of a legislative chamber. In that case, you would not be able to raise a claim of defamation. That is because the law regards comments made in the course of legislative debates as privileged, or immune from suit. Your remedy if a lawmaker damages your reputation during debate is to seek to unseat him or her during the next election. That lawmaker enjoys an absolute immunity from suit. The law justifies this immunity by reasoning that robust political debate is best served by creating a safe place in which just about anything can be said. An absolute immunity is one not requiring a use of judicial discretion to apply. The context makes clear that immunity is applicable.

Qualified immunities require a judge to decide to apply them. Qualified immunities are the great engine of conservative judicial activism. During the past decade or so, federal judges from one end of the country to the other have used grants of qualified immunity to keep cases against police officers from going to trial. Here's how qualified immunity works: If a police officer stops you on the street for no reason apparent to you, you might consider bringing a lawsuit against the officer to deter other offices from doing the same thing. You might claim, for example, that the Fourth Amendment's prohibition against unreasonable searches and seizures makes unlawful a police officer's decision to stop you just because you are, let's say, an African-American in a white man's neighborhood.

But the officer might claim that he had some articulable suspicion that you were up to no good. In that case, if a judge finds the officer had reason to believe you were behaving suspiciously and the officer can put that suspicion into words by saying his decision to detain you was something more than a hunch, a judge will most likely find the decision to stop you lawful. Given the almost infinite variety of locations at which police officers stop folks, context is key. A person looking longingly into a jewelry store window with a suspicious weapon-sized bulge in his waistline is a prime candidate for a search, but how about the kid who whispers "Praise Allah," before boarding an airplane? How about the black teenager driving through his upper middle-class enclave? Is a brief detention by an investigating officer justified there?

The law of qualified immunity says that a police officer is entitled to immunity from suit unless his conduct violates clearly established law or unless reasonable police officers do not agree that his conduct is lawful. In lay terms, police officers get the benefit of the doubt in a close case. But what is a close case?

I get scores of calls each year from folks who are angered by a police search. They call telling me their rights have been violated. Yet as I listen to those folks, I am aware of all the exceptions there are to any legal rule that looks black and white to a layman. While the Fourth Amendment requires a warrant to search or seize a person's papers and effects, our courts have riddled the amendment with so many exceptions to the warrant requirement that the words of the Amendment are now almost meaningless.

During the past 10 or so years, federal judges have decided thousands of cases resulting in the dismissal of lawsuits against police officers. In these cases, a judge reads an affidavit or deposition of a police officer, and then reaches the conclusion that the officer's decision was close enough to the line of legality to entitle him to immunity. Although the Fourth Amendment begins with a presumption in favor of liberty, our judiciary has turned the Constitution upside down. Judges now grant immunity routinely unless the party suing can force a police officer to admit he or she acted without legal justification or in such a way that previous court decisions make it clear that the conduct of the officer was prohibited.

Each year, the Practising Law Institute in Manhattan holds a two-day seminar for lawyers in federal civil rights law. Prominent practitioners, professors and judges teach the classes. Participants in the program receive a two-volume book. Fifteen years ago, the two volumes contained a brief article tucked away in the back of the second volume on the Court's treatment of qualified immunity. It was a relatively esoteric doctrine rarely used by the courts.

Two years ago, the entire second volume of the book distributed to seminar attendees, all 1,084 pages of the book, was devoted to qualified immunity. Each page contained citations to cases decided in every federal court granting immunity to state actors in cases in which the officers were sued for violating the constitutional rights of ordinary citizens in claims ranging from wrongful death to unlawful stops of motor vehicles. The explosion in a legal doctrine designed to increase the power of police officers to act with impunity was accompanied by no popular vote or amendment to our Constitution; it was cooked up by a judiciary that decided there were too many lawsuits against police officers. These immunities are judicial creations designed and intended to keep we the people from evaluating what goes on in the streets by the men and women we pay to protect us.

When is the last the time you heard a politician complain about this judicially sponsored encouragement of a police state? They don't complain. Neither do you. Expanded police power makes us feel safe against terrorists, criminals, and all the things that go bump in the night. But the problem is that as police power grows, so shrinks our sense of liberty and autonomy. Why are you yielding your freedom without a fight?

CHAPTER 3

WHO ARE THE CRIMINALS IN CRIMINAL COURT?

The criminal courts are a place of terror. People walk in; they do not always walk out. Lawyers play high-stakes roles, arguing about the meaning and significance of events long-since past. Witnesses swear an oath to tell the truth and then are submitted to searching and sometimes searing examinations. They do their best. The judge sits atop this smoldering volcano, doing her best to keep passions under control and to guide the roiling emotions down the law's well-worn channels. But the most terrified people of all are jurors. It is up to them to make a decision that will transform lives. Is the defendant guilty or not guilty of the crime charged? We say we trust them with the truth-finding process. But do we tell jurors the truth?

The sad fact is that we don't trust jurors with the whole truth and nothing but the truth. The result is a criminal justice system out of control. We the people don't get justice; we get a body count. Most of us never give this a moment's thought. When you pick up the morning's paper or turn on the television to see a news anchor read his lines, you feel horror about the man accused of abusing his child, the murderer next door, the war on drugs being waged at the corner of every neighborhood. You feel all this until it is either you or a loved one charged. Only then do most folks really stop to consider what our courts routinely do to people. By then, it is usually too late to do anything. Your neighbors no longer care about you. In the brief period of time it takes to make an arrest, you are transformed from citizen to criminal.

Our Constitution proclaims that we are all innocent until proven guilty. This is the criminal law's starting point. Do you really believe in it? Or isn't your view more nearly that a person arrested must have done something wrong? Don't you believe that where there is smoke there is fire?

One of the most difficult criminal cases I ever had involved the deaths of two small children. They were killed in a head-on automobile accident. When the state prosecuted their mother, who was driving the car in which they were passengers, I was outraged. Her surviving child, who was also seriously injured, needed her. Why victimize the surviving child? But the state believed the mother had been drinking before she got behind the wheel of her car. So the state charged her with manslaughter. During plea negotiations prosecutors insisted that she go to prison for five years or so. This result struck both the client and me as unbearably cruel and harsh. We elected to go to trial, reasoning that even if we lost the case, the judge would most likely impose a prison sentence less than what the state offered as a plea bargain.

At trial, the state offered evidence of a blood test taken when the mother was admitted to the hospital just after the arrest. It showed that her blood-alcohol level was well over the legal limit. But when we confronted the state's toxicologist with information about the woman's injuries, including the fact that her liver had been lacerated on impact and the fact that the hospital's testing method failed to distinguish conclusively between blood-alcohol and the contents of a normal liver, the jury acquitted her of manslaughter. She was convicted of one crime: failing to have her youngest child in a child-restraint device. The judge permitted her to go home. There were great tears of joy in the courtroom that day.

Was justice done?

The fact is that the mother had a drink or two on the day her children were killed. It was the Fourth of July. She spent the day with her family at a picnic. We acknowledged that she had consumed alcohol, thus accounting for the scent of it on her breath when the emergency medical staff arrived at the accident scene. We produced witnesses from the picnic, all family and friends, who testified they did not see her consume the amount of alcohol it would have taken to produce the blood-alcohol level detected at the hospital. Quite frankly, the jury could easily have convicted her if it had wanted to do so. The jury held this woman's, and her surviving child's, life in its hands. So did I.

I trust jurors. I think they genuinely try to do the right things and for the right reasons. I wonder why judges and the courts so distrust them.

In Connecticut, where I practice law, jurors are not permitted to consider what punishment a person faces. All jurors are permitted to do is decide whether the state has proven its case. The sentencing consequences are left to the judge. At the very moment a prosecutor is asking a juror to hold a defendant responsible, or accountable, for his acts, the jury is acting in a void that deprives it of any meaningful accountability.

Consider the case of a young man I will name Joshua Brown. He was charged with possession of narcotics with the intention of selling them, a crime punishable by up to 20 years. The case was not strong for the state. Police officers claimed they saw a young black man hand something to another man in a "known-narcotic" area, a law-enforcement euphemism for almost any urban location in which young men of color congregate. It was dark outside. The uniformed officers walked up to the two young men, and one of them fled. In law enforcement parlance, this evidence of flight is what is known as consciousness of guilt, meaning that only guilty people run when they see a police officer coming their way. Assumptions are powerful things.

The officers stopped Mr. Brown, asking him for identification. He handed them his wallet, the officers said, and then ran like the wind. They never caught him.

When the police searched the area near where the two men were first seen, they found a baggie containing crack cocaine worth about $25. One of the officers said he thought he saw one of the young men, he could not recall which one, drop the item to the ground when the officers made their presence known.

An hour later, Mr. Brown called the police department to report that his wallet had been stolen. Later than night, the officers possessing his wallet learned that the owner of the wallet they seized was on parole for another offense. They went to the address on the driver's license. Mr. Brown was arrested when one of the officers recognized him as the very man who had fled after handing the wallet over.

Mr. Brown was all of 23 when he first came to see me. His mother was with him. She insisted he had been home with her throughout the entire evening. The police had made a mistake. Someone else had her son's wallet.

Mothers are never good witnesses. It is axiomatic among criminal defense lawyers that family members are not good alibi witnesses. But when the boy's father turned up as well, together with telephone records suggesting that the boy had been on the telephone with his girlfriend at the very moment the officer's seized the wallet, I was listening. So was the state.

The vast majority of criminal cases are resolved by way of plea bargaining. This is an often misunderstood process. Both parties make an assessment of their respective cases and what they think the case is worth. The concept of worthiness is common to both lawyers in the criminal justice system and used car salesmen. Give two experienced lawyers the facts of a given case, some basic biographical information about the defendant, and the defendant's criminal history, and odds are that both lawyers will come to a similar estimate of what a reasonable plea bargain looks like. Worth, in this instance, is gauged in terms of whether the client should go to prison, and, if so, for how long, together with such other conditions as the length and terms of any period of probation. By way of example, I commonly challenge a prosecutor to write down on a blank sheet of paper his estimate of what a plea offer should be at the same time as I write down mine on another sheet. Almost invariably our numbers resemble one another. It is uncanny, this acquired ability to place a value on the liberty of strangers.

In Mr. Brown's case, the state conceded that identification of Mr. Brown as the man observed on the street was an issue. Although he was on parole, it was for a non-drug-related offense. The state was willing to give him a break. Although possession with intent to sell crack cocaine is a serious offense, it offered him a jail sentence of two years if he would enter a plea. Mr. Brown's mother went to pieces. "He's innocent," she insisted; he wants his trial. Mr. Brown himself was a man of few words. We rejected the offer and elected a trial by jury.

Jurors rejected the testimony of his family and girlfriend, concluding that the police officers had the right man. He was convicted.

What should this young man's prison sentence be for this offense? The state thought that a sentence of two years was just before trial. What trial tax would the state seek to impose to punish this man for relying upon the presumption of innocence and demanding his right to be tried by a jury of his peers?

Connecticut juries are not permitted to make sentencing decisions, except in death-penalty cases. So sentencing in this case was the judge's decision. When he imposed a sentence of 18 years in prison for this offense, my client sank into the chair beside me. His mother began to shriek, and ran from the room. She was intercepted before reaching a door that led to the balcony. (We were on the fifth floor of the New Haven Superior Court.) As I watched marshals subdue her, I turned to see her husband, who was leaning against a wall, clutching his chest. I lost three people that day: one to a long prison sentence, and two to ambulance rides. The case still haunts me, now nearly 20 years after the fact.

Should the jury have known that the state thought the case was worth two years before trial? Settlement negotiations are never admissible as evidence. There is a fear that knowing the party's settlement posture will influence a decision.

It is difficult to believe that a jury would have found this young man guilty if it knew he was going to be locked away for almost as long as he had thus far lived. Shouldn't jurors also be held accountable for what they do?

All cases are subject to the corrosive process of plea bargaining, but the public has no knowledge about the process. That's because the bargaining takes place behind closed doors. In Connecticut, the process of judicial pre-trials permits lawyers to meet alone with a judge to decide what terms and conditions best resemble justice. These meetings are secret. By the time a deal is struck and announced in open court, the work is done. The Devil's been given his due and the parties go through an elaborate choreography, making a record that can withstand appellate review just in case one of the parties later develops buyer's remorse. I've often wondered why there is not something like a public ombudsman sitting in on the plea bargaining process. If justice is supposed to be blind and transparent, why are we hiding the real work of justice, where the scripts recited in open court are first created?

Not long ago, I tried a case for the second time. Both trials, including jury selection, took about a month each. The jury could not agree on whether the state had proven its case the first time around. So the case was tried all over again. This second time, the jury concluded the state failed to prove the crime charged, but convicted my client of a lesser-included offense. He ended up being sentenced to a term of imprisonment close to what he had been willing to plead to long ago. Why were these trials necessary? The victim's family wanted the trials. Just why are we permitting private acts of vengeance to supplant the hard work of justice?

The case arose out of truly horrible facts. My client, Mike Collins, shot a woman point-blank through the head in his kitchen one night. He then shot her friend in the chest, and pursued her down a hallway when she ran away in panic. But for a jammed gun, he might well have killed her, too. After his gun jammed, he ran, turning himself in to the police about ten days after his family had retained my office to represent him.

I recall well learning of this case. I was in Seattle in the Left Bank Book Collective when my cell phone rang. A young associate reported that Mr. Collins' family had called. Two women had been shot; one was dead at the scene. "Is the other woman likely to die?" The bookstore clerk's head turned on overhearing that. The murder of two or more people at the same time is a death-penalty offense in Connecticut. It appeared as though the second woman would survive her wounds. The charges would be murder and attempted murder.

Mr. Collins was a quiet man of few words. He'd previously had trouble with the law, and knew now that he was in big trouble. The court imposed a $2 million bond, and he sat in prison while we prepared for trial. We had to request that he be moved from one facility because angry family members of one of the victims worked at the first prison to which he was assigned awaiting trial.

The story was sad, an example of how a few bad moments can come not just to end one life, but to transform another horribly. Mr. Collins and the woman he was living with, Jill, had three young boys. Jill had a drug problem, and Mr. Collins was worried about whether she would succumb to the oblivion of addiction. He was fighting to keep her in the boys' lives.

When she came home one night at about 1:30 a.m. with a couple of her girlfriends, Mr. Collins wasn't happy. They had been partying. The threesome decided to go out to a convenience store to buy a package of Dutch Masters cigars. The cigars could be hollowed out, filled with marijuana and smoked, a common enough practice. Mr. Collins didn't want these blunts, as they are known, in his home. He told Jill he didn't want her going out that night. She'd had enough partying. The kids were going to be coming home from their baby-sitter in the morning.

Hadn't she had enough for one night? Jill and her friends decided they wanted those blunts. So as they left the house, Mr. Collins told Jill that if she left, she should not return. He asked for her car and house keys. She placed them on the table, and walked out the door. As she and her two friends were walking down the driveway, he began to throw her clothing onto the driveway.

This was too much for one of Jill's friends, who turned and told Mr. Collins not to behave like a baby. She then marched up to the house, and gave him a piece of her mind, throwing beer at him from a beer bottle she held in her hand. She then barged into his kitchen. The two of them traded harsh words. There was pushing and shoving. Jill and her other friend entered the tiny kitchen. As Mr. Collins backed into the corner of the kitchen, he reached into a doorway leading to a narrow and steep stairway to the basement. He pulled out a pistol and shot the arguing woman once through the head. She dropped to the floor and died almost immediately. He then shot the other friend, who put her hand up, deflecting the bullet away from her heart. She tried to escape from the rear of the house. He ran after her, finding her in the hallway and shooting her again. She fell. As he stood over her, the gun jammed. He choked her briefly and then ran from the house.

Why would he do such a thing? The state's theory was that he was jealous of Jill's friends. It was a ridiculous theory. There was no evidence to support what amounted to the claim that this was some sort of lover's quarrel. We decided to put on a defense of self-defense, itself no easy matter. Mr. Collins was quite a bit larger than the dead woman. But when we got the medical examiner's report, the toxicology report was helpful. The dead woman had enough cocaine in her to kill her; indeed, the medical examiner testified at trial that based on her blood work, he would have concluded that she died as a result of drug use had she not died of a crime of violence. Her blood work also reflected that she had consumed enough alcohol to make her drunk, and that she had consumed one or more Ecstasy pills that evening. Other testimony made it clear she had been smoking marijuana, too. An examination of her body showed she suffered no defensive wounds, and that Mr. Collins' DNA was beneath one of her fingernails. It was apparent to us that she had been the aggressor in the confrontation.

During the plea bargaining sessions, we made clear that Mr. Collins was willing to plead to a charge of manslaughter, but that he would not plead to murder. Under Connecticut law, murder is defined simply as intending to kill another and then killing them. There are no degrees of murder, and premeditation is not a required element of the state's proof. Juries are told that intent can be formed instantaneously. Mr. Collins had authorized us to seek a sentence of 30 years in exchange for a plea of manslaughter, a crime that only reflects an intent to cause serious injury but is accompanied by a killing. We suspected he would plead to an offer of 35 years if we could get it.

We were unable to persuade the state to come off the murder charge, and the judge would not budge off a prison term of at least 40 years. Two women had been shot. This could easily have been a capital case, where, had the state elected not to seek the death penalty, Mr. Collins would have been required to serve a term of life without possibility of parole. When plea negotiations broke down, we went to trial.

The first trial was ugly. I had the one and only Perry Mason moment of my legal career during that trial, breaking down a witness completely. But it sadly did not matter, as the witness was mere eye candy for the state.

When my client fled the scene of the shootings, he went to Martin's house. Martin drove him to another friend's house. It was from there that our client went into hiding. Martin testified that he had driven Mr. Collins to the bus station.

"You just lied under oath to this jury, didn't you?" I began.

"Yes," he said.

"You lied because your life has been threatened, isn't that true?"

"Yes."

"And your life has not been threatened by anyone on my side of the aisle, has it?"

"That's right."

"Your life was threatened by folks sitting behind the state here, the family of the victim, isn't that true?" I pointed toward the rows of family members attending to mourn the loss of a daughter, mother and friend.

"Yes," he said, and looked down.

The sad fact is that this lie didn't matter. He could have driven my client to the North Pole in Santa's sleigh. The legally relevant fact was that my client had fled the scene of the crime. Period. I have never understood why the state called this witness. As is so often the case with prosecutors, waste is a given.

Jurors in the first case could not decide whether my client murdered the dead woman. We argued that he was justified in shooting her. She had come into his home uninvited. She was stoned, and had assaulted him. She was angry. And she was backing him into a tight place. Similarly, he was justified in shooting the second woman. He perceived her coming at him as he opened fire on her friend. The jury convicted Mr. Collins of assault in the first degree for the shooting of the living victim, however.

Because he was a convicted felon at the time of the shootings and should not have possessed a gun at all, the jury also convicted him of illegal possession of a gun. He was sentenced to 27 years in prison for this shooting. No jury was informed he faced such eye-popping numbers. I wonder whether a jury that struggled with whether he was justified in shooting the two women would so easily have convicted if they knew what was to come?

During renewed plea discussions we asked for 35 years and manslaughter. The state insisted on murder. The victim's family wanted that, we were told.

The role of victims' families and victims' advocates in our criminal courts is deeply distressing. We say that no one can be a judge in their own case, and yet we empower victims to opine about what justice requires in all manner of criminal cases. Do we really expect a family ravaged by grief and destruction to make a measured assessment of what justice requires? If we thought that was possible, we would permit private prosecutions, a practice that fell out of favor in the nineteenth century. We say that the administration of justice requires something other than visions of vengeance.

So we went to trial a second time. For my money, there should never have been a second trial. My client was acquitted of murder in this case, but he was convicted of a crime the state tossed in at the last moment as a sort of insurance policy. It was just another example of what criminal defense lawyers call the "heinous crime exception to the Bill of Rights."

The law places the entire burden of proof in a criminal case on the state. The state also selects the charges it wishes to present to a jury. Juries are told that the presumption of innocence alone is enough to acquit a defendant if the state fails to meet its burden of proof. In

Connecticut, all jurors must agree if the state is to procure a conviction. Shouldn't it follow from this that as a result of the state's failure to meet its burden of proof in the first trial, Mr. Collins should be acquitted? Of course it should. But that would be too harsh a result for the state, so the court silently slips a burden of proof into the proceedings, while all the while pretending it has done no such thing. In order to acquit a defendant, all jurors must vote not guilty. In the absence of a unanimous verdict of either guilty or not guilty, the result is a mistrial; in other words, the state fails to meet its burden of proof, but it gets a second bite at the apple. These sorts of asymmetries in the criminal justice system outrage criminal defense lawyers. But no one else truly cares. A man accused of a crime is guilty enough for the public at large.

So Mr. Collins was tried again. The evidence was substantially the same as the first time. (The state did not produce Martin and his unnecessary and immaterial perjury.) This time, the state requested that the judge give the jury a charge on what are known as lesser-included offenses.

Lesser-included offenses transform the pursuit of justice into a dart board: If you can't hit a bull's eye, that's all right, so long as your dart lands on the target. A lesser-included offense is an offense closely related to the crime charged, but, typically, one that is less culpable than the main charge. In Mr. Collins' case, murder, the intent to kill someone and the accomplishment of that act, is far worse than merely intending to cause serious physical injury but causing death. I admit that to most folks these are bizarre distinctions. But plenty turns on these distinctions. In Mr. Collins' case, this fine conceptual distinction was worth about 20 years. The crime of murder carries a maximum penalty of 60 years; manslaughter with a firearm carries a sentence of 25 years to 40 years.

Both the prosecution and the defense have the right to request that a jury consider a lesser-included offense so long as there is some evidence before the jury to justify the charge. The defense often seeks a lesser-included offense when it believes that the state has over-charged a case, but in Mr. Collins' case, we argued justification. He feared that a drug-crazed woman was about to push him down the stairs. It was a difficult self-defense case, but the defense was as applicable to manslaughter as it was to murder. Once we chose that defense, our hands were tied: a criminal defense lawyer who offers inconsistent defenses does so at his client's peril. It did not seem to be much of an argument to say to the jury: "He acted in self-defense, ladies and gentlemen, but if you reject that defense, we ask you to find that he didn't mean to kill her." I am not saying such a defense is always inappropriate, but it certainly did not fit this case.

But why should the state have the right to seek lesser-included charges? The state and the state alone has the power to select the charges. A judge cannot override the state's decision. Many are the times I have seen a judge shake his or head in regret when they sentence a nineteen year old to a term of imprisonment for having consensual sex with a fifteen year old partner who was ready, willing and oh-so able to play. The law calls this statutory rape, and imposes, in my state, a mandatory term of imprisonment of nine months. If the state digs in, there is little a judge can do because the judge has no right to substitute charges. Just why we abdicate control of the administration of justice to prosecutors is a mystery to me. It is yet another way in which the criminal justice system is tilted in favor of the prosecution.

The second jury also failed to reach a unanimous verdict on whether Mr. Collins had committed murder. But it did convict him of manslaughter in the first degree with a firearm. At sentencing, the judge threw the book at the young man, sentencing him to the statutory maximum term of 40 years. That sentence is to run concurrently to the sentence he is already serving, so his total effective sentence is 40 years.

These proceedings were a colossal waste of time and resources. Mr. Collins was always willing to plead guilty to the crime for which he was convicted. He did not want to plead to a murder charge, however. His hope was to serve five years fewer than the sentence imposed. Was all this worth the two months or so it took to try the case twice? Probably not, but the system grinds on heedless of cost or waste. In this case, so long as the state was determined to try Mr. Collins for the crime of murder, there was nothing the judge could do to substitute the charges. The state declared victory in this case, despite failing twice to obtain the murder conviction the victim's family demanded. At sentencing, all spoke of what a wonderful young woman the dead woman was. When I dared to raise the context surrounding the shooting, and the victim's state of intoxication, the tension in the room was palpable. Some truths are inconvenient to tell.

The goals of the criminal justice system are to provide a fair, impartial means of protecting society from the truly dangerous and providing a means of deterring others who might commit a crime, rehabilitating the offender and punishing the guilty. Perhaps it serves that goal. But despite the rhetoric we pride ourselves on about this being the land of the free, we incarcerate a higher percentage of our population and for sentences far longer than our democratic counterparts the world over. There is something wrong with our criminal justice system. I suspect a good part of the problem is that we give too much power to prosecutors and not enough to juries to decide what justice requires. What's more, although judges are required to assure that defendants receive fair trials, judges more often than not work in tandem with prosecutors, deferring to decisions that are often patently irrational and driven by something other than justice.

CHAPTER 4

YOUR RIGHT TO REMAIN SILENT, A PRIMER

If you want to short the circuits of an FBI agent, agree to talk to him, but only on the condition that you are permitted to tape record, or, even better yet, videotape, your conversation. Odds are, the agent will flush a deep red, stammer something about that not being possible, and then bluster with some veiled threat or another. The feds, like most law enforcement agencies, have a policy against electronic recording of statements. There is no good foundation for that policy in law or in fact. Indeed, some police officers will actually arrest you if you try to record what they are doing. The crime? Interfering with a police investigation.

Like it or not, police officers are trained to lie to get what they want. The Supreme Court has sanctioned police deception. We've traveled a long way from the days in which the courts thought it better that 10 guilty men go free rather than suffer the conviction of one innocent man. Today we bend and spread to give the police whatever they want. Police officers are granted broad immunity from civil suit. Exceptions to the warrant requirement increase and expand with the passage of time. Even when the police violate your rights, appellate court judges are tempted to find that the error was harmless. It's a 'shoot first, ask questions later' world out there. Only this time the gang members are wearing badges. Who are the dupes upon whom they prey? You.

It used to be that officers claimed the technology to record statements was not available. I've actually heard this nonsense uttered under oath by officers who didn't have the ability to blush. Why that was the case when Radio Shack carried analog recorders that cost no more than a couple of dozen donuts was a mystery to me, and many are the lawmen I have challenged on cross-examination about why the piddling expense of a recording device was too much to bear in the search for the truth. The fallback position was the law enforcement version of the Nuremberg defense: "I am just following orders. Departmental policy does not require recording. I don't know why the policy exists."

This silliness is even less sustainable in the digital era. Now, most folks carry a recording device on them at all times. Most cell phones have the capacity to record audio; the better ones can even record video. There's really no factual excuse for failing to record.

Innocent men and women are persuaded by police officers to confess to crimes they did not commit. It happens with disturbing regularity. Men and women spend decades behind bars for these crimes. And still there is no hue and cry among lawmen about the injustice of it all. A study by University of Virginia School of Law professor David Garrett demonstrates that dozens of defendants have been exonerated of crimes they confessed to once the DNA evidence in their case was tested. These men confessed to crimes they did not commit. Innocent men, I repeat, *confessed* and they did so after being left alone with police officers who "tune them up" to tell the truth.

Left alone with defendants, especially the mentally infirm, the young and the vulnerable, lawmen can easily contaminate an interview by providing inculpatory information to people being interrogated. At trial, these isolated facts are often dressed up as facts that only the perpetrator would know. A witness' statement is paraded before the jury with great solemnity: no innocent man confesses, the prosecutor intones. Of course, the jury never gets to see the pre-interview shakedown, a process that can often last for hours and during which officers use the skills they have been trained to use to break down a person's will to resist. Those techniques rarely involve a physically bruising "third degree." Today the force used is subtle; it leaves no scars that can be seen. The methods used to break a person down are psychological, and without a recording, no juror ever gets to see what really goes on at the police station.

On the federal level the game has a name: I call it the 302 Blues. You speak to federal agents. There is always a federal agent sitting by taking detailed notes. When the interview is over, this agent writes up a typed report summarizing what you have said. The agent then is ready to testify live and in person against you if you offer testimony at variance with what he types on a pre-printed form called a 302. Just which version of fool's paradise requires us to trust our liberty to the integrity of the FBI? It is a felony under federal law to give a false statement to the feds, whether that statement is under oath or not. "Edgar, Edgar, why has thou forsaken me?" Many a man cried from a cross when wicked lawmen bent the truth to crucify them.

Confession evidence is powerful and damning. A person can be convicted based solely on their confession. Because the risk of a false confession is so great, it seems to me that the state ought to be given a choice: if you want the opportunity to use a person's words against them, you must record the entire interview you conduct with that person not just the pretty part you rehearsed and want the fact finder to see.

This rule avoids the inflexibility of a categorical rule requiring confessions in all cases: there may be circumstances in which a tape recording cannot be obtained, when exigency requires a confession, such as, let's say, in Alan Dershowitz's "ticking time bomb" hypothetical. Save the world if you must, but please, not at the expense of the presumption of innocence.

I say give lawmen choices. But let's protect the accused, too. If the police want to use a confession against a person, then require them to record it. There is no excuse to do otherwise.

In the meantime, don't be bullied. If the cops want to talk, press the record button on your telephone. If they refuse to talk to you with a recording device on by all means save that tape. It might just save you from a lengthy prison term when Agent Feel Good has to explain to a jury why he was afraid of a simple recording of the means he uses to search for the truth. When all else fails, simply remain silent. It's your right. Give it away at your peril. But you must do more than merely remain silent. You must be more assertive than that.

Evoking the right to remain silent by simply being quiet is too ambiguous, according to the United States Supreme Court. In yet another 5-4 decision chipping away at the right of the people to be other than supine playthings for the state, the court recently held that silence, even protracted silence, is no bar to interrogation by police officers.

The ruling in *Berghuis v. Thompkins* hardly surprises. The law tilts increasingly in favor of law enforcement. Such rights as we retain against the government and state actors are eroded in the name of judicial restraint. We're going to repeal the "activism" of the Warren Court if it takes a Gulag to do it.

But take heart. It is still the law that citizens cannot breach the peace of a police officer. In other words, the normal bar against offensive speech applicable to communications between private citizens does not apply to a confrontation between a police officer and a citizen. It's still all right to blow off some steam when the boys in blue come looking for you.

The Supreme Court decided conclusively that you must make it clear and unambiguous to police officers that you want to remain silent. Normal polite conventions, such as refusing to speak, do not apply. You need to spell it out for the cops. Make it crystal clear. Lay it out loud and bold.

So here is a quick street pointer for those suddenly in the clutches of the police: call it Street Miranda. It is not for the faint of heart.

1. Hey, numb fucking nuts. (Male)
    Hey, you ovarian lump. (Female)

2. Read my lips. Look me in the eye. Put the freaking donut down and tape record this so you can't deny I said it later. Are you ready? C'mon, focus. Ready?

3. Fuck off. Kiss my ass. Eat shit. Die. Do anything you want to do, but do it elsewhere because I am not buying your shit. Period.

4. Do I have your attention yet? Am I clear enough for you? Is my tone ambiguous, you reptile?

5. Good. I see I have your attention. Now check your tape recorder to make sure it is working.

6. Although my lips are moving, I do not want to talk to you without a lawyer present. I do not believe you have my best interest in mind. You have the right to trick me, to deceive me, and you have been taught to gain and then abuse my trust.

7. Anything I say, and how I say it, will be used by you to try to convict me, whether I am guilty or not. You will lie, distort and manipulate the evidence to suit your purposes. You have the assistance of the prosecutor without cost to you. Anything you want you can get if your suspicions about me are significant.

8. I want a lawyer because I do not trust you. I want this recorded because I do not trust you. I do not want to answer any more questions until I have a lawyer because you are untrustworthy. Stop looking at me like you just fell off a turnip truck. Shut the fuck up and get out of my face.

9. Am I clear enough now?

Of course, carrying on in this vein has its downside. But it has the benefit of being unambiguous enough for most police officers to understand. I suspect some members of the Supreme Court will undoubtedly struggle with the nuances of carrying on in this manner, but its meaning and import has the benefit of being completely unambiguous.

CHAPTER 5

LAWYERS FOR ALL

"What's the matter with you?" The speaker is a good friend and a well-known member of the criminal defense bar in my home state of Connecticut. "Why are you representing people like that?"

He was calling into question my representation of a former police officer. The cop was fired from his police force after being videotaped pummeling a man during an arrest. We entered a guilty plea to misdemeanor assault and no jail time. After the guilty plea, the client's former employer released the videotape to the press. Then all hell broke loose. More than 100 newspapers and television stations either ran the video or commented on the case.

I've viewed the tape dozens of times. The victim was suspected of using a gun in a road rage incident. He fled from police. When he was stopped, my client thought the man reached for that gun. Rather than shoot the victim, my client pistol punched him. For a few terrifying seconds, he could not tell what the man had in his hands. When he saw the man's hands, finally, he stopped punching. There was also a struggle to get the man out of his car, onto the ground and into cuffs. The use of force in these circumstances was justified, in my view, and I've tried dozens of unreasonable force cases in the federal courts.

But the prosecution thought otherwise. My client was charged with a felony. The tape is shocking and there is intemperate language on it.

There was a risk he might be convicted, hence the plea, which carried no jail time. It was an intelligent means of managing his risk.

But here is the rub: I am a lawyer. I know I have choices and that I am not obliged to represent everyone who walks in my door. But I do not draw distinctions between folks accused of crimes. I represent people accused of abusing children, dismembering bodies, burning down homes, robbing banks; why, shocking to some, I even represent police officers and prosecutors. Everyone needs a defense, and I have yet to encounter a type of case I will not defend.

The sporting view of law pits one "team" against another. At Gerry Spence's Trial Lawyers College, where I taught for a few years more than a decade ago, there was an almost cult-like exclusivity to the program: no prosecutors or insurance defense counsel allowed. That's just plain wrong. "The people" need representation in many contexts. I no more want a person accused of killing a family member to walk free than I want my insurance company to go insolvent paying bogus claims.

Lawyers are mere ambassadors for other people's troubles. Movement lawyers scare me: I don't have causes that transcend a particular case. When my agenda conflicts with that of my client, I may have a conflict that impedes my representation. The self-righteous mob that forms whenever someone stumbles is an ever-present danger to liberty. That mob is most dangerous when it turns to consume one of its own fallen members. But David felled Goliath with one well-placed stone. Trial lawyers learn to find these stones and strike with them. The best fights, the fights that transform lives and hold the state in check, take place in the criminal courts.

One thing that attracts me to criminal law is the sheer romance of it all: I stand alone between my client and catastrophe. "Bring it on," I say, although in the well of the court, a judge's steely eyes replace the glare of high noon, and thinking fast is more important than shooting fast. I love going to court, and I love trial. Sadly, there are not many trial lawyers left in the United States. We're becoming a profession of paper-pushing panderers. The art of the deal is everything. The swagger of the gunslinger is giving way to the swayback waltz of the negotiator.

Not long ago, I defended a man in a capital felony in Connecticut. I did so as a special public defender appointed by the State of Connecticut. The client had no funds for a lawyer.

I do not do much court-appointed defense. Several years ago, I quit the federal Criminal Justice Act panel in protest over the impossible delays and procedures in submitting vouchers. A paralegal of mine was nearly in tears one day when a form had been bounced back from the federal court for a third time. It made no sense to spend dollars of staff time to chase pennies of federal reimbursement. "Take these forms and shove 'em," I said. It felt good saying that. But I was probably wrong to react so.

In the Connecticut case, I was paid the sum of $100 per hour. That may seem like a lot to the non-lawyers out there, but when you consider the staff whose wages I pay, the rent, the insurance, the dues and all the other miscellany that it takes to run an office, the truth is that I lose money at this rate. But it is the top government rate in Connecticut, and, more to the point, the Office of the Public Defender did not wince when I requested additional funds for investigators or experts. I miss the cases from the Criminal Justice Act panel. There is no way my client could have afforded to pay for all this.

All Americans should have the right to counsel at government expense when the government charges them with a crime. We should have a universal public defender system, one to which all Americans can turn for counsel when they are accused.

Prosecutors have virtually unlimited discretion to bring charges, and they are armed with staffs that include not just investigators, but experts from state forensic labs and the efforts of law enforcement at the local, state and national level. Few defendants faced with this arsenal are as well equipped. Were O.J. Simpson a member of the middle class and not a member of the sporting pantheon, I have my doubts whether he would have beaten his murder case.

A universal public defender system does not mean conscripting all members of the bar and making them government employees. It means that all members of the bar can apply to be included on a list of qualified defenders. It also means that making your way onto that list, and remaining there, requires demonstrating minimal competence in the difficult work of defending the accused.

Not all lawyers will seek such appointment. Those who don't want strings attached to what they do can compete for the private dollars. But the middle class, those folks not indigent but without the means to hire a full defense team, won't be facing the resources of the state armed only with the wits of the lawyer they could afford.

The fact is that it is a very expensive thing to provide an adequate defense to a criminal case.

Robert Wilson was charged with conspiring to commit mail fraud and aiding and abetting another to make false statements on a tax return. When he was arrested, he claimed he was broke. A public defender was appointed, and, after a six-week trial, Wilson was acquitted. Only it turns out that Wilson wasn't so broke after all. As a result, the trial court ordered that he repay the government some $52,000 for the cost of his defense.

The cost of defending against allegations of criminal misconduct is typically hard to calculate. Private counsel don't submit bills for public review. Institutional public defenders don't submit affidavits for payments on their cases as the cost of their services are sunk costs: paid regardless of whom they represent and whether they go to trial. I am unaware of any systematic review of vouchers for payment submitted by counsel appointed under the Criminal Justice Act.

In the Wilson case, the court determined that the defendant was one of the world's foremost experts on antique weapons, and that, as such, he had a great earning capacity. It ordered him to repay the costs of his own defense.

Most members of the middle class would be wiped out by a $52,000 legal bill. Like Wilson, they will not have the funds ready at hand and will have to pay them over time. A client convicted of a felony typically loses the ability to make payments on time. Hence, it is a common practice in criminal defense to get payments up front. A criminal defense lawyer never looks quite so alluring as on that first date, when all is hope.

I am no fan of the American Rule, requiring each party to pay their own legal costs regardless of the outcome, especially in the context of a criminal defense. When the government charges a person with a crime, the work of police officers, prosecutors, experts and investigators are all borne by taxpayers. The full weight of the government, with its almost magical ability to finance just about anything by means of taxation, is brought to bear on an individual. Who can match the government's spending and resources in defending a crime? Almost no one.

If the government is going to spend unlimited resources prosecuting a non-violent crime, the government should also be required to bear the cost of defense. In an era of over-criminalization we are all criminals from time to time. The only way to rein in an aggressive government is to require it to bear the costs of the fights it picks. The government should be required to calculate the unit cost of each prosecution: what does it cost to bring an action? And I am speaking here of both the prosecution and defense. Perhaps if Congress were required to count the cost of all the new laws it passes year by year we'd have a little less prosecution of marginal conduct.

At the very least, when the government loses at a criminal trial, it ought to be required to reimburse the defendant for the cost of defense. Otherwise, we make a mockery of the presumption of innocence. We tell folks that they are innocent unless proven guilty and then send them to the poorhouse to vindicate these rights. Is this what is meant when folks talk about the process being the punishment?

Connecticut was the first state in the nation to adopt a public defender system, so we have a tradition of leading the way when it comes to the pursuit of justice. It's time we advanced the claims of justice once again. What's needed now is a universal public defender system. In plain English, each and every person accused of a crime should have court-appointed counsel.

"Public defenders for all? That's preposterous. Think of the expense!" you say.

Indeed, let's think of the expense.

First, we fully fund each and every prosecution. And we do so in Connecticut without even the insulating effect of a grand jury to protect us from prosecutions that are just plain silly. Not long ago, an associate of mine won a criminal case. It arose from a neighbor dispute. The jury acquitted and then expressed chagrin. Why had the state brought this silly claim to trial?

Here are some reasons why the court system sometimes wastes its time. First, state constitutions give victims of all sorts of offenses, large and small, a right to be heard. That means prosecutors are often loath to use their discretion to dump a bad case: it's just too much work to go toe-to-toe with a wound up victim. "Let the jury decide" becomes a means of avoiding responsibility.

Taxpayers fund each prosecution, no matter how grave or frivolous, but the costs of defense are spread unevenly. The indigent get public defenders while those just above the level of indigency are on their own. They must hire lawyers. And they must also hire investigators and experts of their own. The wealthy can match the state dollar for dollar. But those folks in the middle can't. Private lawyers often lament that they cannot hire the experts they would like because their clients are broke.

Why not create a system that funds both prosecution and defense equally? Retain the adversarial system but house it in a single agency. Call it, despite its Orwellian overtones, the Ministry of Justice.

Under such a regime, the prosecution division would be given a budget for each fiscal year, and it would be expected to give an accounting of what it spent prosecuting each case. The defenders division would be given an equal budget; it too would have to give an accounting of what is spent on each case. At the end of each year, lawmakers could see the consequences of the annual expansion of the penal code. Are we getting social utility for each new addition to the list of prohibited acts?

Let's not forget that under the American Rule, the loser always bears his or her own costs. There is something wrong with a criminal justice system that empowers victims, and permits prosecutors to pursue each and every claim for which probable cause can be found. Such a system promotes waste, and invites scorn for the law.

The system I propose requires that the work of seeking justice in the criminal law be funded by the state. It would assure a level playing field in all sorts of cases. Just now, a new bevy of so-called experts are being unleashed on defendants in child sex cases: testifying about such gibberish as incremental disclosure, and delayed disclosure. If the state is going to fund this swill, shouldn't it also finance the defense experts? Isn't there a danger that people of few means will be convicted because they cannot afford to meet the state's case?

Under the regime I propose, anyone would have the right to opt out and hire the high-rolling titans of the bar. But those without means to buy all the bells and whistles would not be whistling in the dark because they have no dough.

A public defender system for all is long overdue. Justice requires it.

CHAPTER 6

FATHERS AND SONS; IS CRIME IN THE BLOOD?

But for a shooting in Detroit sometime in 1954, odds are I would not have been conceived. So I owe my father a special debt for his decision to shoot a man in the Motor City. He fled from Detroit after the shooting and hid in Chicago, taking with him a pretty young woman he had been seeing. She became my mother, and I was born when they settled down in Chicago. It remains an open question whether I would have been conceived, or if he would have tried to settle down, had he not needed to lay low for awhile.

I gather the shooting had something to do either with collection of a fee, distribution of profits or defending my father's right to conduct business in his territory. You see, my father was for many years a professional armed robber. This was after he snuck into the United States crossing from Windsor, Ontario into Detroit sometime during the Depression. He died a few years ago in his mid-eighties. His heart gave out. None of us are sure just how old he was, or, frankly, just what to believe about him. Somewhere along the way he forged identity papers so as to remain in this country. I am the son of an illegal immigrant. This was in the good old days before Homeland Security tried to put the nation on lockdown.

No one told me these truths when they really mattered. As a child, I came to feel my father's absence in the hammering sort of way that death comes. My father simply did not return home from work one night. My mother and I waited for weeks, and then months. When the money ran out, we were run out of our apartment. My mother declared bankruptcy. I was sent to live with relatives who seemed none-too-pleased to see me. When my mother and I were reunited, she seemed distant, somehow. I think my father broke her heart, and such heart as she retained, though filled with love, could beat only half as strong. It is fair to say she was undone by sorrow when I needed her most.

But children never really sense loss. They are too busy discovering all that is new about their surroundings. How was I to know I was, in effect, an orphan when I had hardly known my father? Being a latchkey kid wasn't so bad, either, although on those few occasions in which my mother did not make it home at night and I had forgotten my keys, I learned how difficult it is to get a good night's sleep hiding in a stairwell. Childhood was for me a time of annual moves and roots never quite finding soil. I learned to hide what I did not want taken from me, and that often included emotions. But words are weapons, and I learned to use them well enough.

The words that inspired me the most and haunt me still were in the Bible. I thought the Psalms were written for me. I memorized many of them in junior high school and high school. I do not recall them now, but when I open the Old Testament and see them, it is almost as though I have to restrain myself from falling headlong into their embrace. The hound of heaven still lurks, apparently.

Somehow and improbably I went to college, and then to graduate school, nearly completing a Ph.D., and even teaching for a couple of brief years at Columbia University in New York. But I hated teaching. I wasn't sure there were truths worth conveying. I was restless, looking for trouble, and wanting somehow to find a bigger and better stage. Is it any wonder that I spent nearly five years as a journalist, writing daily editorials for two of the largest newspapers in Connecticut? But even that did not satisfy. I went to law school, and fell in love with the law. The result was chaos for my wife and two children. Like my father, I left young children behind with a mother who seemed ill-equipped for the challenge.

I remarried after getting on my feet as a trial lawyer.

One night as I was preparing closing arguments in a felony murder case, my office phone rang. The caller spoke with a southern lilt, it was not quite a drawl. "I am your father's wife," she said. That weekend, I drove to Virginia to meet a man I had not seen in nearly forty years. He had no apologies to offer for breaking my heart.

He and his father came to Detroit from Sfakia, a port city in southern Crete. They came as so many immigrants do, for economic opportunity, sending money home to the family they left behind. Soon enough, my father was on his own, living by his wits in Detroit. Much though he loved his father, I suppose it is a family tradition to throw the males quickly and too soon into the world to see what they could do. So my father learned English, speaking it flawlessly in no time. He, too, was gifted with words.

As a young man, he quickly learned just how easy it was to perform an armed robbery. Back in the days in which people were paid with cash, it took but a little planning to study the route a payroll truck would take on a Friday, and how a company would prepare to receive the cash. He assembled what he called "my crew," and they would strike several times a year at various points in the United States. By carefully selecting three or four targets a year, they could live free and easy most of the time. He owned an apartment building; "You needed a warrant to ascend further than the second floor;" when "the heat" was on, he and his associates each had "safe houses" to which they would flee. When I think of my father now, I imagine Robin Hood as chief executive officer of a hedge fund. I shudder to think he could have been Sacco or Vanzetti, professional fellow-travelers in the armed robber's world.

It all sounded romantic enough. My father talked like Sam Spade. Was any of it true? Perhaps. Several years ago, I was showing him and his wife around the northwestern corner of Connecticut, a lovely place that is part Norman Rockwell, and part, in those few semi-urban enclaves the state dramatically refers to as cities, David Lynch and Blue Velvet. As we drove through Thomaston, I pointed out an old factory, and started my lecture on how the decline of the brass industry had laid waste to the Naugatuck Valley.

"Isn't that the old Thomaston Clock factory?" my father asked. He was sitting in the back seat of my car.

"Yes," I said, surprised. "How did you know that?"

"Never mind," he said. I saw him look away. I wonder when that factory had been robbed at gunpoint of its payroll.

He was quick to tell me that although he possessed a pistol during those years, he never used it, except once. Most of the time, it was enough merely to brandish it. Few men are willing to risk death for another man's cash.

But one night he did use it. He was vague about why he did, and whether he killed or merely wounded, the man. All he would say was the feds wanted to talk to him. So he decided to flee Detroit and head for Chicago. He was seeing a pretty young dark haired woman at the time, a smart enough woman who hadn't finished high school, but was longing for better things. She became my mother in due course, once they had settled into a love nest all their own. My father tried to live what he called "the straight life" in the Windy City. He hung in for a few years working long hours and hustling. I recall visiting him once at his office, where he was superintending a phone bank of women, all apparently trying to sell magazine subscriptions. My father had a gift for gab, and, I suspect, an eye for the ladies.

As he tells the story, he learned that he had a rare blood disorder. He was afraid he was going to die. He did not want to be a burden to my mother and to me. So he left, hoping to find a quiet place to fade away. I believe this about as much as I believe that Santa Claus left me all those presents as a child. I think the truth was more than my father could face. It was never his idea to reunite with me. His wife found me, spotting me on Good Morning America one day as I discussed a case.

The straight life was no doubt too much for him. I get that. I see young clients who have made fast and easy money in the drug trade try to shift gears and hunker down behind the counter at Burger King. Whoppers just don't cut it when you can make thousands of dollars a week selling crack.

So off my father went, trying to return to the life. But his contacts were gone. He was getting old. He settled in Virginia and began to work in group homes for troubled teens. When he told me this, my heart broke. I could have told him all he needed to know about trouble. I know what it is to bury my face into a pillow and to wrap it tightly around my head so as to howl and weep in rage and sorrow.

I will never know how much of what he told me in the couple of visits I had with him as an adult is truth, and how much is romantic fiction. I know that he wanted me to lie for him. His new wife was a Mennonite.

He wanted me to assert that he and my mother had never married, as though I really knew the truth about my parents' relationship. And when his wife once asked me about my sister, I was floored. I grew up as an only child. And I confess to wild hope of unearned fortune when his wife asked me whether the trust fund he had set up for me had cushioned the blow of his loss. I would have bought a farm in Vermont if that money truly existed. My father covered his tracks well. I guess he needed to do that.

When he died, I turned up at his funeral unexpectedly. He did not want me to know he was failing. But his wife told my daughter, so there I was, suddenly, in a Virginia funeral home, and then at his grave. Many of his in-laws did not know I existed. It was painful to be an interloper at my father's funeral.

His wife and I sat at the graveside and watched his coffin lowered into the earth in Williamsburg. I clutched her hand and wept. I had lost so much when he walked out of my life. Now I was losing him all over again. A man spoke at my father's funeral. An old friend from Detroit, I was told. He spoke platitudes and never so much as mentioned the family my father left so many years before. I kept my distance from the stranger, and he did not seek me out. I suspect he possessed many more secrets, but I wonder, still, whether he, any more than my father, was prepared to tell the truth.

I relay this short version of a chaotic youth not to inspire pity. I am capable of generating more than enough of that for myself. But this story defines so much of what I became I cannot help wondering about the fates and furies lurking just out of view. I am my father's son. A man ill at ease with responsibility, forever on the move, and living somehow in the shadow that respectability casts. This explains, I tell myself, why I will always side with the despised man in a fight. They are the ones who need lawyers, just as I needed a father.

I suppose the lack of a father also explains why I find myself again and again falling within the orbit of great and powerful men. I'll never stop looking for the father who was absent when I needed him most. Like it or not, his absence marked me. My adult children feel the loss; I simply do not know how to be a father, so I sit by and hope that a loving heart is enough. While I remained present in the lives of my children, I was not a constant presence. I console myself with the thought that I did a better job than my father did. I remain hopeful that my children will do even better.

Such bad luck as I endured as a son has been more than compensated for by the mentorship of some great lawyers. John R. Williams of New Haven broke me in, teaching me all he knew about civil rights litigation and criminal defense. Gerry Spence shared generously of his insight into stories and the psyche. And F. Lee Bailey has taught me a healthy awe of common facts. I remained with John for a dozen years; I broke painfully and publicly with Gerry when I worried that I would never escape his towering shadow. Only with Lee did I enjoy what approaches an adult relationship.

I visit Bailey from time to time. He is generous beyond my merit with his time and talent. Bailey is incisive in an almost brutal manner. He pushes hard and is candid with his disdain for the artless question or lazy response. Bailey's self-confidence is brash; his mind is like a meat cleaver, slamming away at loose joints.

Spence is quite different. He displays no confidence. Whereas Bailey pushes, Spence beckons. My sense is that if on the dock at Heaven's gate, Bailey would spit into the eye of St. Peter, demanding the front of the line. Spence, by contrast, would hang back, eyes down cast and tear-filled. Spence has as great an appreciation of facts, but he works harder than anyone I know to root facts into a pattern that summons a helping response.

I'd like to see a trial pitting Spence versus Bailey. Their styles could not be more different. Indeed, so different are they that I cannot imagine them as co-counsel in a case. I believe that when O.J. Simpson was shopping for counsel he found his way to Spence's door. The Wyoming wizard turned him down, so Simpson went with the dream team of which Bailey was a part. At least that is one version of how it went.

Bailey and Spence radiate different forms of energy: Bailey is an intellectual centrifuge, pushing all boundaries to their limit; Spence is centripetal, drawing all to himself. I resisted Spence's pull to the point of alienating him, a fact I accept with regret.

The differences between the two men are reflected in their paradoxical surroundings. Bailey's office is a place of clean lines, with everything in its place. Orchids decorated the place on my recent visit; simple elegance standing watch as a mind went about the brutal work of open heart surgery without the use of anesthesia. Spence seems most comfortable on his ranch, a place of elemental and therefore brutal natural energy, yet his is a gentle intensity. Each man seems to surround himself with outward trappings holding in relief their defining characteristics.

I have spent long hours considering what makes Bailey a great lawyer in a manner altogether different than the form of Spence's excellence. I have catalogued what I have learned from each, and worried as I always do that I cannot measure up to the standards of the men I admire, even as I fear them.

But I have been given a great gift, the gift of their time freely given. I accept these gifts without worrying about whether I will use them well, or even at all. Both men are legends in American law, and both are aging. I am lucky to have gotten to know each. But now the challenge is to take what they have taught and make something of it. It makes me look forward to the next trial: these men have survived much and done much, so much more than I have or most likely ever will.

I admire great trial lawyers. There are so few of them anymore. Amid the clatter of lawyers pushing and shoving to show what they know, few have anything to teach. But somehow, in some secret cavity hollowed out the day my father walked out the door, I still crave a father's embrace and presence. I won't get that from Spence, or Bailey, or Williams, or even from all the Clarence Darrow memorabilia I have begun to collect, or from my signed copy of William Kunstler's biography. Like any lawyer, I will have to learn to walk alone, singing my own song, often in great fear and terror of what a jury will do to the person who has placed their life and hopes in my hands. The sound of my own footsteps still sounds lonely. I wish my father had remained at home when I needed him most.

CHAPTER 7

EXPERTS FOR SALE

I am a cultural popular illiterate, it seems. That's because I work long hours and prefer the company of a good book to the glare of a television set once I finally make it home. The result is that I've missed the revolution in thinking about crime and the criminal courts fostered by such shows as *CSI*. But I hear about these shows in courtrooms daily. Everyone is talking about them. Both the prosecution and the defense worry about something called the "CSI Effect."

We say that trial is a search for the truth, but the fact of the matter is that trial is often far from the truth. The parties summon the witnesses they can locate. These witnesses bring their biases, interests and perspectives to a courtroom. Questions are put to the witnesses by the lawyers, judges rule on what is and is not admissible, and then juries are told to deliberate and make a decision. But trial resembles a game of blind man's bluff. We learn each year just how tenuous a jury's judgment can be. The Innocence Project has thus far used DNA evidence to secure the release of hundreds of innocent men and women from the nation's prisons, many of them convicted based on erroneous eyewitness testimony. It's terrifying, or at least it should be.

The rules of evidence are intended to assure that only reliable evidence finds its way into a courtroom. In general, evidence comes in two forms: direct and circumstantial evidence. Despite folklore to the contrary, courts regard circumstantial evidence as every bit as reliable as direct evidence. Therein lies one of the hidden dangers of the CSI Effect: jurors are inclined to give the state the benefit of the doubt on questionable claims so long as those claims are dressed up in the guise of expert testimony.

Direct evidence is sensory evidence. What did a witness see, hear, smell, touch, or, in the most bizarre of cases, taste? This is evidence of facts delivered to the senses. If you are capable of reading this book, it is almost certain that you are capable of testifying as a fact witness.

The proof of a crime often involves far more than mere proof of an event that can be perceived. Most crimes require the proof not just of a prohibited act; also necessary is proof of a culpable mental state. We lack the means to observe the contents of other minds. We permit jurors to draw inferences about mental states and facts by means of circumstantial evidence. Here's an example to fix the distinction between direct and circumstantial evidence forever in your mind.

You see thick black smoke passing by the window of your office on the tenth floor of an office building. Is there a fire? You see no flames; what you see is the product of a fire's combustion in a form you associate with actual flames. It is a logical and reasonable inference that where there is smoke there is fire. Hence, the law would permit you to draw the inference that somewhere below the tenth floor there is a fire.

But suppose the fellow in the office on the eighth floor was a madcap inventor testing his new smoke machine, a product he was asked to design by some super-secret government agency as a means of disorienting enemies on battlefields? In that case, your conclusion that there was a fire below would be erroneous. Logical though it is to believe that there must be a fire, in fact there is simply some Oz-like gizmo belching out the deceptive vapors. In that case, the reasonable conclusion simply isn't true. One danger of circumstantial evidence is that jurors draw perfectly reasonable but erroneous conclusions.

I realize that my example is far-fetched. But I chose a dramatic example to illustrate a simple point. Circumstantial evidence can be rational but wrong. Consider the following use of circumstantial evidence to prove that a man was sane at the time he strangled his wife to death.

Greg M. was a skilled draftsman with a seemingly ordinary enough upbringing. He followed in his father's footsteps and took a job at a Connecticut defense contractor. The work could be stressful, and as Greg got older, he became more and more withdrawn. In his early thirties he also became convinced that his wife was cheating on him with his colleagues. When he finally snapped, he was admitted to the psychiatric unit of a local hospital for treatment. The hospital released him but noted on his medical record at the time of his release that it regarded him as a potential threat to others. The hospital could easily have sought to keep Greg on a psychiatric hold, but that would have involved extensive legal proceedings.

Several months after his release from the hospital, Greg strangled his wife to death in the kitchen of his home. After doing so, he drove to his parents' home, telling them he had done something horrible. Hours later, he surrendered peacefully to a police SWAT team. He seemed calm and lucid to the arresting officers.

Greg was charged with murder. His trial lawyer hired a forensic psychiatrist to evaluate Greg. The doctor determined that the man was mentally ill and that he lacked the capacity to conform his conduct to the requirements of law at the time he killed his wife. Greg's trial lawyer had him enter a plea of not guilty by reason of insanity.

Murder is what is known as a specific intent crime. Connecticut law defines murder simply: the intent to kill a person and the actual killing of the person. It is distinguishable from less culpable forms of homicide based on the mental state of the defendant. Manslaughter, for example, is intending to cause serious physical injury but actually causing death; it can also be the taking of life as a result of a reckless act, an act the defendant knows carries a serious and unjustifiable risk of death or serious injury. These forms of killing are more culpable still than negligent homicide, which involves the taking of a life as a result of an act of gross carelessness. These fine distinctions between murder, manslaughter and negligent homicide turn on circumstantial evidence of an accused person's mind: you just can't see intent, recklessness or negligence. Juries are told they can decide what is going on in a person's mind. It is a dangerous and tricky business, carrying great and grave consequences: a person convicted of murder might well serve a sentence of 50 or even 60 years. However, criminally negligent homicide carries a penalty of only one year in prison. A sentence of not guilty by reason of insanity requires a defendant to be remanded to the state's psychiatric hospital where he is held until he is deemed sane and no threat to the community. The state hospital is a lot like the Hotel California: once you check in, it is rare that you are permitted to leave.

The state's cross-examination of the psychiatrist who examined Greg was simple: was Greg able to drive from the home in which he killed his wife to his parents' house? Yes. Did he surrender without incident once the SWAT team arrived at his parent's house? Yes. Did he appear calm and lucid when he surrendered to the police? Yes. The state argued that all these factors were circumstantial evidence that the man was not insane; if he could do all these things shortly after he killed his wife, surely he was capable of controlling his conduct within the limits the law requires. The state did all this without calling a psychiatric expert of its own. Greg was convicted of murder.

I took Greg's appeal to the Connecticut Supreme Court. That court upheld the conviction. Greg is serving a sentence of what will undoubtedly be the rest of his life for an act he committed one morning. The finding that Greg was legally sane at the time of the killing stands.

Jurors are routinely told that they are free to accept or to reject the testimony of an expert. In Greg's case, a jury rejected the opinions of one of the state's most respected forensic psychiatrists based on a common sense conclusion that a guy able to drive his car and not foaming at the mouth at the time of his arrest was sane when he killed his wife. Shouldn't the state at least have been required to have an examination of its own conducted? I worry that it did not because it feared the result should its expert conclude Greg was insane at the time of the killing.

Of course, it is possible that Greg's expert was full of hot air. The use of bogus expert testimony is a significant problem in the criminal courts. A recent study by the National Academy of Sciences laid waste to the use of forensic sciences in the courts. A whole new line of attack is forming on the use of experts.

The National Academy of Sciences' report on the forensic use of science, *Strengthening Forensic Science in the United States: A Path Forward*, warns that much of what passes for science in the courtroom is not very reliable. Much though we rely on showmen such as Connecticut's Dr. Henry Lee, known to most Americans for his work in the O.J. Simpson trial, to dazzle us with conclusions and inferences draped in the sort of drama Sherlock Holmes might appreciate, the academy's conclusion is simple and direct. "[L]awyers and judges often have insufficient training and background in scientific methodology, and they often fail to fully comprehend the approaches employed by different forensic science disciplines and the reliability of forensic science evidence offered in trial."

There really is no such thing as forensic science. There are core sciences and applied sciences. These techniques and methods of investigating things yield results that are more or less reliable. Calling something forensic merely means it has been prepared in anticipation of a court proceeding.

I recently cross-examined a forensic toxicologist. On direct, he could not throw the word forensic around often enough. On cross-examination I asked him whether he agreed with me that calling a science forensic added no scientific value. He said he would have to think about it. After questioning him on other topics, he later agreed. All it means to call something forensic is to say it was prepared for use in the "forum," or court. There is no scientific method known as forensic. The public is seduced by the fancy sound of the word.

The academy suggests that courts and juries are often hoodwinked by fancy rhetoric. I recall a case of mine years ago involving bite mark evidence in a murder case. The state's forensic odontologist relied on digitally enhanced photographs of the victim's breast in claiming that my client had bitten her. When I challenged the expert to tell the court how a digitally enhanced process had translated the three-dimensional curve of the victim's actual body into the two-dimensional image of the victim's breast, the expert could not. The court permitted the testimony, saying it went to its weight, not to its admissibility. When the Supreme Court later ruled that it was error to admit this testimony, it was too late: the Court found the error harmless. It was an early example of the

CSI Effect: throw a guy in a lab coat in front of a bunch of jurors and let him rip. It hardly matters what is said. Judges fail when they admit into evidence questionable opinions and then avoid responsibility by asserting that the jury must assess the weight of the evidence. Most jurors, and most lawyers, don't know enough science to question an expert's pronouncement. The new NAS study suggests we all need to do our homework and fight a whole lot harder to keep junk science out of the courts.

Truth, we say, wins out at trial. Well-prepared adversaries in the well of a court each pressing as hard as they can for their client will yield shimmering gems, compacting coal into diamonds, glittering truths that will decide facts. Such is the theory anyway.

But junk science poses a challenge to the adversarial system. Is the legal community up to the task of testing truths generated by science?

We all know that courtrooms are not laboratories. But when a scientist takes the stand to testify, when he enters the forum and by dint of taking an oath turns his science to forensic use, do lawyers and judges advance the search for truth, or do we get in the way?

One proposal for reform is shocking in its elegance: the creation of an independent National Institute of Forensic Science. Among its many tasks would be the establishment and enforcement of standards for the collection and interpretation of forensic evidence. "Scientific and medical assessment conducted in forensic investigations should be independent of law enforcement efforts either to prosecute criminal suspects or even to determine whether a criminal act has indeed been committed. Administratively, this means that forensic scientists should function independently of law enforcement administrators," the NAS report states.

This is heady stuff. Imagine a forensic laboratory housed, let's say, in a state's Department of Public Health, and administered by scientists accredited in forensic work. A non-accredited person would not be permitted to give scientific testimony in a court. We'd need to rework the legal standard for admissibility of scientific evidence to reflect that general acceptance of a method does not entitle a mere apprentice without scientific training to opine. The present state of things permits a police officer to testify about a machine's test results without the ability to comment on why or how the machine does its work. This so-called black box testimony is routinely permitted by the courts and it comes down to the following tautology: it is reliable because we rely on it.

The current state of forensic use of science—can't we ban the term "forensic science" once and for all as meaningless?—is dismal. Law enforcement crime labs interpret data and testify on behalf of the state or Government. There are no Public Defender labs. And private labs are either too expensive or too poorly equipped to provide much assistance to many defendants. The NAS study acknowledges that observer bias plays a role in the current use of scientific testimony by law enforcement. What you see often depends on where you sit. If you are sitting in the FBI crime lab, small wonder the defendant looks guilty.

The report goes on to acknowledge an obvious truth. I've often been in trial and seen prosecutors put experts on the stand without apparent comprehension of the science on which the expert opines. It is easy to cross-examine these experts if you do your homework and read their texts: the state often does not, and hence rehabilitation of the experts fails when a bleary-eyed prosecutor stands deer-like staring into the headlights.

The courts are awash in the forensic use of science. Often the experts are employees of law enforcement agencies offered as witnesses by prosecutors. The science is often of questionable vintage. They appear in court before jurors dazzled by mere mention of the term "forensic." They testify as defense counsel chips away with what remains of a high schooler's understanding of chemistry or physics. Juries sit back, puzzled, dazzled and confused by a vocabulary not even the judge really understands. How many people are convicted by jurors who say, in effect: "I'm not sure what all that meant, but it sure sounded good"?

The NAS report is a sub rosa challenge to the adversarial system of justice. Perhaps the truth does not emerge in every case. Perhaps there are cases in which the lawyers, who are supposed to be gladiators well equipped to slay cant, misperception and error, don't know enough to ask the right questions. Perhaps truth is sacrificed by judges who throw up their hands and say if it is good enough for others it is good enough for me, without ever really asking if the others know what they are talking about.

I favor the adversarial system of justice because it highlights my principal skill as a lawyer: cross-examination. But I wonder whether an inquisitorial system might not better serve. Science does not thrive in a world built on conflict; the search for truth is collaborative and bound by a common method and norms. Are these methods and norms in perpetual conflict with the ethos of a courtroom?

It sure felt as though Alfred Swinton was convicted of murder based on bogus science. The jury convicted him of murdering Carla Terry. The key piece of evidence against him was bite mark evidence. Photographs of the decedent's breasts were digitally transposed into an electronic image. Mr. Swinton's dental impressions where taken and then transposed onto an acetate overlay. The two images were then laid one on top of another and compared. A forensic odontologist then compared the images and pronounced them a match. The match was far from persuasive looking – ill-defined bruises corresponded to locations of teeth. They looked like bite marks, all right. But whose?

I represented Mr. Swinton at trial. I did not challenge forensic odontology as junk science. Under the liberal standards governing the admission of scientific evidence, the so-called expert had the requisite skill, training and experience. And the field had been recognized in other judicial decisions. I challenged whether the expert could give any meaningful account, or foundation, of how two-dimensional images were translated into digital pixels. The trial court disagreed. When the Supreme Court later considered the issue, it found admission of the evidence to be harmless error.

I might not have pressed hard enough for Mr. Swinton. Consider what the NAS report had to say about science in the courts. "With the exception of nuclear DNA analysis ... no forensic method has been rigorously shown to have the capacity to consistently, and with a high degree of certainty, demonstrate a connection between evidence and a specific individual or source."

The academy singles out forensic odontology as particularly unreliable. "Although the majority of forensic odontologists are satisfied that bite marks can demonstrate sufficient detail for positive identification, no scientific studies support this assessment ..." Question: then why are we allowing it into evidence?

Don't ask Dr. Henry Lee or anyone at the University of New Haven this question. Notably absent from the list of persons on the NAS panel is the ubiquitous Dr. Lee. It was a curious omission. Neither he nor any member of the forensic science laboratory he established at the University of New Haven was on the panel that drafted the report. I suspect that is because they were all too busy either fundraising or testifying in courtrooms. Dr. Lee is the most recognized forensic scientist; recognized to television court watchers nationwide. Why wasn't he put on the NAS panel?

Here is what I am afraid happens to jurors seduced by the CSI Effect when the state offers forensic expert in the case of so-called "shaken baby syndrome."

More than once I have heard a prosecutor in trial urge a judge to admit contested evidence: "The state cannot prove its case without this evidence, your honor," the argument goes. To which I typically respond: "So what?" The rules of evidence require reliable evidence. The trial deck is not supposed to be stacked in favor of conviction.

But the deck is so stacked. And few judges seem prepared to do much about it.

This is rarely so clear as in the case of expert testimony in cases with no victims, or victims who cannot testify. In such cases, the evidence of a crime must be circumstantial: there are no eyewitnesses who can describe the event. Circumstantial evidence, evidence of things seen permitting an inference about things unseen, is, despite television warnings to the contrary, as probative as eyewitness evidence.

But this business of drawing inferences is dangerous. A jury can draw the wrong conclusion and send an innocent man or woman to jail. It happens in cases alleging so-called "shaken baby syndrome." In such sad and tragic cases, an infant dies. A medical examiner finds burst blood vessels in the infant's eyes, bleeding around the brain, and a swollen brain. This fateful trio is a sure sign that the child came to violence at the hand of a person who had cared for it, the prosecution contends.

Each year, more than a thousand infants die and present with such symptoms. Their mothers, fathers and babysitters are then investigated, and often prosecuted. Hundreds of custodial care givers are now in prison because of the presence of these symptoms.

The sad fact is that many of these folks are innocent. These symptoms can occur in the absence of criminal conduct.

The American Academy of Pediatrics recommends that the diagnosis of "shaken baby syndrome" no longer be used. In the language of the law, the diagnosis is a result of junk science: flawed methodological premises yielding unreliable conclusions. Uncannily, the pediatricians' findings reflect a general tendency in the scientific community to reject much of the science that is routinely admitted in a courtroom to prove a defendant guilty.

So why are the courts so quick to admit questionable scientific evidence?

I suspect the answer is that the state could not prove many of its cases without junk science. In others words, we sacrifice the presumption of innocence on the altar of something akin to scientific voodoo. We do this because of a concept with which psychologists are familiar: act hunger.

Only stones are unmoved by the sight of another's suffering. Every heart is inspired to act in the face of life's great tragedies. A deep-seated hope harbored by all is that of an orderly universe. We want things to happen for a reason. When things occur that inspire pity or horror, we want to restore the hoped for balance. That requires righting what was done wrong. In the criminal courts, that means assigning blame. Thus, when a child dies, there must be a culprit. In a secular age, we prefer a defendant, as many of us have long since retired the Devil as an efficacious moral agent.

But acting merely to relieve an inchoate sense of threat is not justice. We should care as deeply about assigning legal guilt to people who have done nothing wrong. A disciplined criminal justice system would refuse to admit junk science at trial and leave the human tragedies that serve as the fodder for criminal trials unresolved. In other words, good courts reject junk science but frustrate the innate impulse to find a villain in every sorrow. The urge to act all too often yields an overreaction.

The next time a prosecutor intones that contested evidence is necessary to prove the state's case, I'd like a judge to say, simply: "What has that to do with justice?" Let's face it: sending a person to prison for decades rarely accomplishes anything.

CHAPTER 8

WHITE COLLAR WOES

I have a confession to make: I've always been wary of the white collar criminal defense bar. Real criminal defense lawyers defend those accused of murder, rape and other crimes of violence, right? I mean, wassup with the pinstriped suits and the Grey Poupon sensibilities of those with money to burn? Isn't white collar work for momma's boys and wannabes?

Harvey Silverglate slapped me silly and forced me to see just how wrong I am. His *Three Felonies A Day: How The Feds Target the Innocent,* is a tale told from the trenches by a white collar warrior worthy of any courtroom. It may well be that the threat to liberty is greatest in the world of white collar crime, where prosecutors armed with vague laws, investigative grand juries and seemingly infinite resources can crush virtually anyone, regardless of whether the person has committed a crime.

Silverglate practices in Boston and writes a column for *The Boston Phoenix*; he is a sixty-something lawyer and litigator who managed to survive Harvard Law School without losing his street smarts. I've never met him, but his photograph on the dust jacket of the book bears an uncanny resemblance to Robert Fogelnest, former president of the National Association of Criminal Defense Lawyers, and now an expatriate living in Mexico. Fogelnest is a good friend, so I suppose there is a danger that I read too much into Silverglate's feisty prose, but I don't think so.

Economic hard times make populists of all who struggle, people who then yield to the temptation to indulge in a sort of populist dualism, separating the world into good and evil. The current bad guys are Wall Street bankers, those smarmy folks who packaged derivatives, traded them like baseball cards among themselves, exploited the Barnum-like quality in each of us that wants something for nothing, and then crashed the economy. We're enraged, most of us, that these banking bandits pulled this off and still got a free ride from the government. What a country: the rich get rescued by government and ordinary people are forced into bankruptcy.

It plays, doesn't it? This neo-populist rage slips easily off my tongue. Tar and feather the leisure class, I say.

Silverglate warns against this easy anger. It is the sort of thing that prosecutors use to fuel prosecutions of doctors, lawyers, businessmen, salesmen, bankers, virtually everyone who, in this complex and regulated economy of ours, sell goods and services under the watchful eye of the government. Each can be prosecuted on a whim; all of us are criminals when viewed through lenses tinted just so. In the world of white collar crime, the crimes of mail fraud, wire fraud and obstruction of justice become fall back crimes prosecutors can allege when all else fails: these offenses are so broad and sweeping by definition that almost everyone is guilty of them at some time or another. Many defendants choose to enter pleas rather than fight costly and expensive wars that might well vindicate them but at the expense of bankruptcy.

A friend recommended *Three Felonies a Day* when he learned I was representing a lawyer in an ongoing federal investigation. I told my friend how terrifying the investigation was. When questions were raised about one topic, I met with the feds to address them. I provided documents that rebutted their suspicions that anything was amiss. They acknowledged that they did not know about the documents and I assumed the case would be closed and all would return to normal.

How naive.

You see, the government wanted to turn this lawyer into a witness against another lawyer. So it spared no expense to try to terrify my client. Federal agents visited his neighbors, his favorite restaurants, his clients. The agents behaved like organized crime goons, flashing badges and guns in an effort to scare up evidence of any kind of wrongdoing that they could dream up. Why? They want my client to flip, criminal defense speak for testify, against someone who is the real target of their ire. There are reputations to be made in high-profile prosecutions, you see. The feds were trying to "climb the ladder," as Silverglate calls it, using my client as a rung. The trouble is, there was nothing for them to seize upon. So they bullied, blustered, and threatened. When challenged, they hid behind the veil of grand jury secrecy: the spectacle disgusted.

But Uncle Sam wanted his man. So his agents dogged my client, sending almost daily reminders of their ability to root through all the electronic trash they could find: banking records, credit card receipts, old tax returns. They will press until they find something they can use as a club to bludgeon my client. All this with the aid of a secret grand jury, a body that was intended to protect liberty but now serves as the American equivalent of Stalin's secret police.

I've handled white collar cases before, cases involving government employees, bank employees and those alleged to have abused positions of trust. But, frankly, I did not see the political significance of each of these prosecutions clearly enough until I read Silvergate.

The defense of a crime of violence is challenging. Jurors are terrified by glimpses of a frightening world. Stepping across the divide separating law-abiding jurors from the blood and gore of the event alleged is difficult. Jurors look upon the allegations as they would upon a foreign culture.

But in white collar cases, there is no divide. When the government can accuse anyone of a crime and the crime is simply engaging in business, or taking advice from a professional, we are all potential defendants. The gap between juror and defendant is eliminated. What is evil now is not the blood on the murder weapon. No, what is evil now is the secret hand of a federal agent, lying, intimidating and insinuating his way into our lives. White collar work, Silvergate persuades, is one of the front lines in the battle against abuse of government power.

Silverglate radicalized me. There is no mob quite so dangerous as a self-righteous mob, and populism is the rage of the day. White collar defense is less the work of those who don't want to get blood on their lapels than it is a world in which spreadsheets and ledgers become the new Molotov cocktail. And anyone can be a witness turned now to the government's purposes, even your spouse.

The Securities and Exchange Commission recently elected to pursue a claim against David Zilkha, a former client of mine, for insider trading, after settling a similar claim against his former employer, Pequot Capital, for a whopping $28 million. The financial press was agog. The investigation of the claim was first opened, then closed, then opened, then closed. Senators raged. There were suspicions that people in high places quashed the truth. But for an angry ex-wife, the SEC would never have pressed its claim against Zilkha.

Pequot Capital was accused of insider trading by using information obtained from an employee of Microsoft; the employee, David Zilkha, later worked briefly for Pequot. Federal investigators closed the case amid claims of a cover up.

Then, in 2009, all hell broke loose in the divorce proceedings involving Zilkha and his ex-wife over who got to visit with their children and when. During the divorce proceedings, it came to light that Zilkha settled an employment claim against Pequot Capital. The SEC got back in the game when it received a copy of Zilkha's computer hard drive, allegedly containing damning emails between Zilkha and a former employee of Microsoft. The hard drive contained an email that sure seemed inculpatory. Pequot quickly settled the SEC action against it, going out of business, and paying a penalty of some $10 million together with some $18 million in monies clawed back from its allegedly unlawful gain. The agency then pursued administrative claims against Zilkha in a forum that denied Zilkha the right to conduct discovery of just how, when and for what purpose, the SEC was givne the hard drive.

Permit me to shed a little light.

When I represented Zilkha, there were bitter court proceedings about whether and under what circumstances he would see his twins. It was a legendarily bitter custody dispute by Connecticut standards. In the course of that dispute, he disclosed receipt of settlement proceeds from litigation against Pequot, which had fired him shortly after his employment, began. He was later compelled to disclose the source of those settlement funds.

Apparently, before the couple headed to divorce court, his now ex-wife downloaded a copy of his computer hard drive. That was in 2004. Whether she left an intact copy of the data in the computer is an open question. From 2004 until 2009, the ex-wife presumably kept a copy of the hard drive, or entrusted someone else with its safekeeping. The hard drive did not find its way into the hands of the SEC until Zilkha filed motions in the family court to see more of his children. The timing of the disclosure of this data coincided nicely with what we believed to be his ex-wife's apparent strategy of doing everything possible to keep Zilkha from seeing more of his kids.

At the time the hard drive found its way into federal custody, Zilkha's ex-wife retained separate counsel to handle her appearances before federal investigators, including, I believe, the FBI. At or about this time, negotiations took place about whether Zilkha would withdraw his custody-related motions. It was represented that he would be in a lot of trouble if he did not. Zilkha did not stand down in the fight to see his children. Shortly thereafter, United States Senator Arlen Specter was on the floor of the Senate demanding that the Pequot investigation be re-opened based on "newly discovered" emails in the case. Those emails, I am certain, came from the downloaded hard drive. The SEC apparently finds no shame in being pressed into service in a custody dispute. Indeed, the agency paid the ex-wife a tidy $1 million tax-free bounty for her work. She is a member of the bedroom whistleblower brigade, a new breed of white collar shock troopers long welcome in places such as Stalin's Russia, now rewarded by tax-free bounties in this the land of the free.

My sense is that the SEC opted for administrative hearings in this matter to deprive Zilkha of the discovery rights he would otherwise have had if the case had been handled in the District Court. Zilkha may never have the right to test the well-founded hypothesis that his ex-wife, or someone acting with her knowledge and consent, caused the hard drive seized in 2004 to find its way into the SEC's hands as part of a full-court press to keep Zilkha from focusing on the fight to see his children. The SEC, in short, became a pawn in a bitter family-court custody dispute. Zilkha was ordered to pay a fine.

Were I a Wall Street worker subject to SEC regulation, I would raise questions about federal investigators raiding the boudoir for evidence against me. I'd be outraged that my ex-wife could potentially use material she took from me during our marriage as leverage in a custody dispute. I'd be appalled that this game could be played, and that my ex could keep the kids, and get a bonus to boot. But most of all, I would be disgusted that the SEC would seek to hide its tracks by depriving me of the right to discovery.

Transparency, we say, is important in the regulation of the financial industry. But is there no transparency about the regulator's activities, and to what depths they will descend when it turns its sights on the regulated? When the day ends and I engage in a little pillow talk with my spouse, should I assume that the SEC is sharing our bed?

Or consider the business of recruiting witnesses, another pastime of ambitious federal prosecutors. The feds call these witnesses cooperators, or concerned citizens. The defense bar calls them snitches or rats. The feds make unusual bargains to get these witnesses to turn on others. Behold the pathological case of Michael Seifert, whom the feds tried to recruit against Martin Minnella, a long-time criminal defense lawyer and client of mine in Waterbury, Connecticut.

Sixty-year-old Seifert was cooling his heels awaiting trial on one of the many bank robberies he was alleged to have committed in the greater Waterbury area. I'm sure there was an innocent explanation for it all. But he needed to offer that explanation to then Waterbury State's Attorney John Connelly.

Seifert's best defense appeared to be the United States government. Uncle Sam want to help Seifert. You see, Seifert did the feds a favor. He expected the government to perform its end of the bargain. Seifert's fondest hope was that federal prosecutors would charge him with bank robbery and that the state would drop its charges. Then the feds could meet in secret with a federal judge and Seifert's lawyer, former prosecutor turned court-appointed defense lawyer Brian Spears, to cash in on a cooperation agreement. Seifert most likely would not walk away from these crimes, although he could. He prayed no doubt for entry into the Witness Protection Program and a fresh start in another state. But Seifert certainly faced better prospects in the federal system, where prosecutors can talk about the substantial assistance Seifert gave to the government.

Call it *attempted* substantial assistance in this case. You see, Seifert tried his best, with the assistance of obliging FBI agents, to entrap Minnella into saying something inculpatory about Connelly. If all had gone according to federal plans, Minnella would have promised Seifert the world, telling him that in exchange for a lot of cash, his old buddy John Connelly would take care of Seifert. This is the federal script that agents had been running around the state auditioning witnesses with for more than a year. They contacted Minnella's former and current clients looking for potential stars. We kept track of these interviews as best we could. All were cloaked in secrecy, and our every question about the antics of federal agents was met with a claim that what they do is part of a grand jury investigation and is therefore secret. It is supposed to be hush-hush, super-duper secret Justice Department stuff. Try talking to the feds about this tidal wave of defamatory swill and you'll be lectured: "we don't talk about our investigations."

The trouble is that when Seifert talked to Minnella, the lawyer did not recite the entrapping lines written for him by eager federal agents. Call it a bad day of fishing for the feds.

But didn't the feds promise Seifert they would help him if he would try to trap Minnella and Connelly? It appears so. So Seifert's lawyer asked Connelly to drop the charges against Seifert.

Connelly had a conflict in the government's view, and should have been disqualified. What conflict?, Connelly asked. But the government would not talk about the conflict. That's because they don't talk about their investigations. So Connelly would not drop the charges, and the feds would not say why they think there is a conflict and Seifert, the man who hoped to be queen for a day, was trapped between two sovereigns and looking like a fool.

Seifert's lawyer informed Judge Richard Damiani that the man had been cooperating with federal authorities for well over a year. Doing what, pray tell? Wiring up to make recorded calls to Minnella? Recruiting other prisoners as part of a federal casting call? Are grand jurors ever told about all the chum thrown on prison waters in an effort to drag these two men down? Do grand jurors ever learn of all the potential witnesses who laughed at the fantastic claims agents sought to press into the form of facts? Oops, that's confidential. We the people can't be trusted to know what work reputation's assassins do when they troll the state, banging on doors, suggesting unpleasantries such as potential tax audits or disclosures of marital infidelities to the recalcitrant witness.

We've come a long, long way from the era of the founding of the United States. Federal grand juries, which were once a means of protecting people from the infamy attendant to being investigated for a crime, are now the secret tool prosecutors use to rummage with subpoenas through virtually every area of our life. Fear of the unknown has become a prosecutor's best friend. Prosecutors play on that fear, claiming all the while that grand jury secrecy is sacrosanct.

No one is immune: prosecutors might reach out to talk to you. There are suspicions that you have broken the law. You retain a lawyer. Your lawyer speaks to federal prosecutors to get a sense of what's going on.

At this point, you have several choices. Obviously, if you are the target of such an investigation, you have every reason to want to know the nature of the allegations being leveled against you. You press for information. "Grand jury secrecy," the prosecutor intones and he says little. But this is really little more than self-righteous swill. The government is pouring through the offal of my life and it must keep secret what it is doing to me? The history of the grand jury is rooted in a different source: a grand jury was supposed to protect a citizen against the abuse of government power. Today the grand jury has been transformed into an investigative Star Chamber.

It is not uncommon for lawyers faced with a pending investigation of their clients to attend what I call a "show and tell proffer." You sit with a prosecutor and a "special agent" or two of the FBI—practice pointer, all FBI agents are "special." The government lays out in general terms the evidence that it thinks supports criminal charges against you. At this point, you can either respond to the claims or not.

If you choose to respond, your lawyer will insist that you do so under cloak of what is known as a proffer agreement. This is a contract. The government promises not to use your words against you; you promise to tell the truth. All bets are off, however, if you lie. Then you can be prosecuted for making a false statement to federal officials. That's what happened to former Illinois Governor Rod Blagojevich.

Making a false statement is far different from a perjury charge; your statement needn't be under oath, as is the case with perjury, it merely need be on some material fact and made to a federal official acting within the scope of his or her duty. The feds can often make something of nothing by scaring the wits out of a person at a proffer, and then prosecuting them for lying when all else fails.

Barry Bonds was charged with lying to a grand jury about his steroid use. (He was under oath then.) Roger Clemens also was charged with lying to Congress about his steroid use. (He, too, was under oath.) Marion Jones, a gold medal sprinter went to prison for lying to investigators. And now there are reports that the Postal Service bicycling team, the star of which is Lance Armstrong, is under federal investigation and may face charges of fraud, drug distribution, tax evasion and money laundering. Expect a few counts of lying to be tossed in as well. As a general rule, and with few exceptions, it is wise to plead the Fifth whenever the government comes calling. There is no telling how your words will be used against you. The government gets to lie, bob, weave, and engage in all manner of deception. Yet, if you do the likewise you go to prison. Did We the People consent to be governed by a caste of professional liars?

Prosecutions for making a false statement would be less frequent with a more transparent grand jury process. I am not suggesting that the grand jury should be opened to public view. What I am saying is that a process that was intended to protect citizens from over aggressive government officials should be open and transparent to those targeted for prosecution. Using grand juries to develop secret cases against folks and then playing hide and go seek with the truth when interviewing targets is obscene; it reeks of Stalin, not Jefferson.

The early stages of a federal investigation are steeped in fear. A target hopes against hope that someone will listen. A target hopes that by being candid, the government will understand. But candor is a one-way street in this secret process. Too often, grand juries are used as secret tools to rebut the claims made by targets in proffer sessions. Frightened clients are inclined to trust and hope that a true word will deflect the secret ambitions of prosecutors looking for new scalps to mount on their walls. The temptation to waive the Fifth Amendment and speak at a proffer is great.

It cannot be good law to permit prosecutors to use secret grand juries to unearth awkward half-truths about a person and then not tell the person about these misperceptions while there is still time to avoid the train wreck and expense of a trial.

I am increasingly inclined to take a hard line about discussions with the federal government on my client's behalf. If the government is going to be coy about speaking the truth, then it seems prudent to consider seriously whether they deserve the right to speak to my client at all. Sure, the risks of silence can be great: misperceptions can yield a trial, with all the risk that entails. But I'd rather let a jury sort out the truth than play cat and mouse with a government that has turned the use of grand juries on its head and has transformed them into a secret chamber of terror.

Don't grand jurors ever revolt and ask the prosecutors tending them behind closed doors why the other side isn't present to offer its point of view? I doubt it, and besides, if they did, the government would keep that secret, too. Silverglate was right. There is a war going on all around us. It is taking place in the world of accusations of white collar crime.

CHAPTER 9

BLACK MEN, WHITE JUSTICE

I've never been comfortable walking along the color line. In 1967, when the city of Detroit went up in flames, I watched soldiers drive up and down our street on the East Side. Angry white men sat on the porches of modest blue-collar homes armed with weapons. If the "jigaboos" came to our neighborhood, these men were going to shoot first and ask questions later. I was terrified by the prospect of being overrun by strangers. When the kids in our neighborhood were scooped up and sent to a summer camp at Harsen's Island, not far from Detroit, I was relieved. We sat by the poolside of the camp listening to a radio trying to determine whether our neighborhood had gone up in flames. When we got home from camp, I was surprised to find paratroopers still camped out on the baseball diamond near our home. Violence seemed near at hand. I was rooting for the white guys in this conflict, the people who looked like me.

Years later, I attended graduate school at Columbia University in New York City. The campus overlooks Harlem. I went to Columbia to study the history of political ideas. Based on what I had seen in Detroit, it did not seem to make sense to study the law. How could our nation survive the racial tensions and injustices that were so self-evident? It seemed better to study philosophy and the history of ideas. Why study the rules that bound a society together if that society's conflicts and tensions would soon yield its collapse? Several of us sat one hot

July evening overlooking Harlem; we wondered why the city wasn't in flames. How could it be that a people could be so abused and not revolt in violence? I felt the burden of my skin and its associated privileges. Sure, I had come out on top of the social heap. But wasn't all the moral energy in those oppressed? Although I would not have chosen to be born a person of color, I was envious in an odd sort of way. Being oppressed would mean freedom from some lingering sense of guilt. But Harlem simmered in silence.

This sense of ambivalence about race has followed me through the years. Not surprisingly, it colors my perspective on the law. I am a white man in a criminal justice system that still treats men and women of color as though they are slaves. I enjoy the privileges my profession affords, but still look with something like envy on the lot of those liberated from a sense of guilt. I keep waiting for the fire next time, the fire that will never come.

I was forced to confront my racial ambivalence when Henry Louis Gates Jr. was arrested in Cambridge, Massachusetts. The Harvard professor was arrested at his home as a result of a senseless confrontation with a white police officer. The conflict between the two men was both inevitable and unnecessary.

First, some fundamentals: Professor Gates is a PBMWA, as in professional black male with an attitude. In a public statement released by his lawyer, Charles Ogletree, Gates set the tone for what went wrong in Cambridge. Gates had just returned from spending a week in China, where he had been filming a PBS documentary entitled "Faces of America."

When Gates got home from China, the door to his home was jammed. He and his driver worked to force the door open. The two men were spotted in the act of forcing the door by a passerby who did not know them. She called 911 about a potential break in. A lone officer arrived. The caller was present at the scene and reported that two black men were apparently forcing the door of a private residence.

The officer, whose stilted police report reads like a bad example of someone struggling with English as a second, or perhaps third, language, reflects the demeanor and attitude of a cop who thinks "trust and obey" is written into one of the Constitution's amendments. Sergeant James Crowley, who is white, comes off as arrogant. The postscript to his report could easily read: "If he had only followed my orders I would not have had to arrest him."

Pride versus arrogance was on display at the Gates home. This is the sort of quotidian conflict that takes place daily in almost every community. A little insight on behalf of both parties could have avoided the commotion.

It was broad daylight at the time, so eliminate the uncertainty that comes with the dead of night. Sergeant Crowley was still outnumbered. He walked to the home's front door. There is no question that he was well within the scope of his duties. He was trained to approach cautiously.

Gates saw the officer approach. According to Gates' statement, he refused to step outside when asked to do so by the officer. Gates told the officer he lived there and that, by the way, he taught up the street at Harvard. Gates is mightily impressed with himself.

Gates turned from the door to go to his kitchen to retrieve his wallet. Crowley followed without objection. Gates provided identification to prove that he resided at the home. Gates then asked the officer for identification; the officer never told Gates who he was or whether there were pending charges against Gates. Gates was steaming now: the nerve of this man, investigating a potential crime at my castle! I teach at Harvard!

According to Gates' statement, he followed the officer to the door where he was astonished to see other officers. While at the door, he was placed under arrest. Apparently, the charge was disorderly conduct. Under Massachusetts law, disorderly conduct involves "fighting or threatening, violent or tumultuous behavior, or creating a hazardous or physically offensive condition for no legitimate purpose other than to cause public annoyance or alarm." It is hard to see how Gates' conduct, petulant though it was, rises to that level.

Crowley's police report paints a different picture. Gates accused him of being a racist, did not comply with the officer's request for identification and escalated his rhetoric to the point where onlookers were alarmed. In this version of events, Gates broke the law.

Was Gates guilty? We'll never know. Cambridge prosecutors gave him the Harvard kid-gloves treatment and bowed to Gates' wealth and status: charges against Gates were dropped without so much as a court appearance. In spite of his race, Gates got privileged white-guy treatment.

If Gates believes his rights were violated, he ought to bring an action for unreasonable entry and false arrest under the Fourth Amendment. But Ogletree is too good a lawyer to believe such a suit would be easy pickings. There is little doubt that Crowley was present at the home in response to a complaint. He had a right and duty to investigate the complaint. Indeed, Gates' decision to ignore the officer's order to leave the home could easily have exposed him to arrest.

Was there justification for the arrest? According to Crowley's report, Gates stood on his porch yelling at onlookers and berating the officers before his arrest. While it is generally true that you cannot breach the peace of a police officer, it is also the case that behaving poorly in public can earn you a set of handcuffs. If Crowley's report is true, Gates' purpose may well have been to try to create public alarm. The arrest may well have been justified. It is the sort of claim that has qualified immunity written all over it, at least insofar as a civil action is concerned.

Like it or not, when police officers are called to investigate a potential burglary those present in the home have some minimal duty to comply with police orders. That might not feel good to a globe-trotting Harvard professor grown fat and sassy playing the race card, but it is the law.

Gates was wrong. Crowley wasn't much better. And President Obama looked more than a little foolish inviting the two men to the White House for a beer or two. Thousands of Americans face these sorts of tense confrontations every single day in the United States. Some of these folks end up dead, as did Oscar Grant, a young black man who was shot to death by police officers in San Francisco.

But for the fact that Gates is well connected and famous the case would not be remarkable.

What drove this case to the headlines was not race. The defining element was socio-economic class. Poor black men get pushed around all the time, and no one cares.

When my clients get arrested for contempt of cop and charged with some minor offense such as interfering with an officer, or, if a member of the general public was within earshot, breach of the peace, no one outside the courtroom cares. These cases are typically resolved quickly and quietly, but the Gates case was different.

Ogletree's book, *The Presumption of Guilt: The Arrest of Henry Louis Gates Jr. and Race, Class, and Crime in America,* taught me much, but not about the law.

It is black letter law in every jurisdiction that a person detained by the police, even wrongfully detained, must comply with the officer's commands. Stepping outside to discuss the matter was not the constitutional outrage Gates thought it to be. The Fourth Amendment is not an instrument of protest during a police seizure. Gates was a fool to escalate the confrontation, even if he was the sort of fool I would root for each and every time.

Crowley, of course, was a bigger fool. He was disrespected in public, and by a black man, no less; in another time and place, Crowley might have lynched the man. But this was 21st century Cambridge. No noose was handy; Crowley used the tools at hand to make his point: handcuffs and the power to arrest.

This arrest was inevitable, even if unwise. As Ogletree points out, in this confrontation, at least at the outset, Gates' race trumped his class. He was arrested for being black and proud in his own home. There is something deeply offensive and wrong about this.

So far, so good, and so obvious. But Ogletree fails really to grasp the significance of this confrontation. He claims to represent Gates. It is unclear whether that representation was in any civil capacity. For Gates' sake, I hope Ogletree did not advise him civilly. Not once in this book does Ogletree mention the havoc the doctrine of qualified immunity has wrought on claims of false arrest or illegal seizure arising under the Fourth Amendment and brought under cloak of 42 U.S.C. Section 1983. This pernicious doctrine gives the benefit of the doubt to police officers in a close case. Gates' case is such a case.

The real story in this case is not that Gates was arrested. These sorts of arrests take place daily in the United States and are perfected against people of all races. The real story is the use to which this arrest would have been put if Gates were not a good citizen, buddy of the president and a Harvard professor. Had Gates been a young black man on probation, the arrest might well have signaled a violation of probation proceeding, without benefit of a jury trial or even a suppression hearing to test whether the evidence against him was lawfully obtained. A person without means and influence would have been asked to stipulate to probable cause or pay a small fine to make sure the police were covered in the event of a civil suit. Gates got the Donald Trump treatment. Class mattered in this case, and was dispositive.

I fault Ogletree for writing half a book, but I still recommend the volume. The epilogue is a lengthy set of reports from black men about their experiences with racial profiling, harassment and misperception. Reading these reports was deeply moving and a present and necessary reminder that the color line still separates and divides in ways that are intolerable. It is perceived to be a crime in many parts of the United States to drive while black; skin color matters to investigating officers.

Ogletree is right to shine a light on race and racism in the criminal justice system. But the light he shines has been dulled by too many years behind a lectern preaching to the choir where he, like Gates, opines. He needs to spend more time in a courtroom getting his ass kicked from one end of the room to the other to speak with the sort of raw energy necessary to inspire battle. I am not moved to man the barricades on behalf of the leisure class.

Ogletree suggests that eliminating peremptory challenges, the practice of excusing otherwise competent jurors for strategic reasons, might help eliminate racism during jury selection. Perhaps. But it is so hard to get a case to a jury that I would still rather have challenges as a tool when selecting a jury. I would be willing to make a deal with the Devil if he were so inclined—I'll give up peremptory challenges if we can also eliminate qualified immunity. Let's let the people decide constitutional cases and tell us what they think of the law. I trust them more than I do judges and the academy. Juries live on streets the professariat only talk about.

I've never met Charles Ogletree and odds are I never will. My heart aches at hearing about the role of race in the many miscarriages of justice that take place daily in this country. My heartache is compounded by the sight of a court system that has created legal doctrines to excuse all but the most blatant and obvious forms of misconduct. That Charles Ogletree, a Harvard professor, could write an entire book on a garden variety arrest and miss the legal significance of what went down makes my heart ache even more.

Racial tension terrifies me. I was 11-years-old when Detroit burst into flames as a result of racially animated violence in 1967. The violence seemed about right to me. Detroit was a racist shit-hole. So you might think I am nodding a sort of "I-told-you-so" smile over Omar S. Thornton's bloody rampage in Manchester, Connecticut. Accused of stealing beer from his employer, a beer warehouse, the young black man was ushered into a meeting with union and management. Resign or be fired, they told him. He took a gun out and shot the place up, killing eight people before killing himself.

I was in a court about 30 miles from Manchester when news of the shooting broke. No one thought race then. Someone had gone postal at a workplace. Thoughts turned to jilted lovers and disgruntled employees.

These sorts of events happen, and the roots of the violence are usually mundane.

Before he killed himself, Thornton spoke for about four minutes with the Connecticut state police. The 34-year-old man told the officer: "this place here is a racist place." Family members told the press in the wake of the shooting that Thornton had long felt victimized by both his employers at the Hartford Distributors, and by his union, the Teamsters, on account of his race. Both union and management deny racial harassment.

When I first learned that the shooter was black and all the victims were white. I worried in a plantation-owner sort of way about copy-cat crimes. I have represented many people of color in employment-related disputes. Anyone who believes, even for a moment, that the color line is not alive and well in the United States lives in a dream world. There are simmering tensions. There is black rage and white resentment. The "N" word is often spoken in hushed terms.

Attorney General Eric Holder is dead right: we are too cowardly to meaningfully discuss race in the United States.

Even so, I am not prepared to excuse Omar Thornton's rampage. He is not the warrior Malcolm X pretended to be. If every dispossessed Omar Thornton in the country were armed and took aim today at noon, the country would be no better off by 1 p.m. As deeply satisfying as it must have been in some rage-soaked way for Thornton to shoot and kill, this rage merely destroyed: it built nothing other than a castle of sorrow and caskets of shame. One of those caskets contains Omar Thornton today.

I don't know whether Omar Thornton was a thief. I do know he was a murderer. And I do not know whether his employers and union were trying to sell a little Jim Crow with their Budweiser; it wouldn't surprise me if they were.

I do know that race matters in the United States. A person's life chances are determined largely on the basis of socio-economic class. Many people of color live the legacy of slavery. The result is an economy and society composed of many different Americas. The privileged and talented get great rewards. Those less fortunate are forced to settle for far, far less: too often the line between haves and have-nots corresponds to the color line. A person forced to the margin, whether white or black, will come to believe that the current regime of laws, institutions and social conventions are illegitimate. Omar Thornton apparently lived on the other side of the line dividing haves and have-nots.

I suspect there are millions of Omar Thorntons out there, fuming at the vast gap between the rhetoric and the reality of American life. For many folks, that gulf is cast in racial hues; for others the chasm is purely economic. But for all there is a lingering sense that there is something askew in a nation that promises equality for all and then denies so much to so many.

I suppose some part of me still awaits the conflagration that never came in 1967. Will there be a fire next time? Or maybe we will continue to shuffle along, promising more than we can deliver, and incarcerating millions who just can't get it right because we won't let them. I enjoy my side of the color line. I wonder why we permit the line to exist. Perhaps we have no choice, although I suspect we do.

CHAPTER 10

THE WAR AGAINST DESIRE

I'm not sure just why the American public always seems to need some unifying demon to hate. At various points, we've turned our rage on alcohol, people of color, Communists, and, now sex. Somehow, a stark contrast between good and evil seems to satisfy in a way that beholding shades of gray does not. Are good Americans required to be Manicheans?

We are in the midst of a moral panic and suffer from a syndrome later historians might well call sexophrenia. We use images of sex to sell everything from toothpaste to cars. Yet once someone takes the sales pitch a little too seriously, we lock them up and throw away the key. It's a form of madness to which we have succumbed before.

In the mid-twentieth century, Sioux City, Iowa, gay men were regarded as perverts, and, hence, ready to snap. The city's children needed protection from what right-minded people thought the men might do to children. A new wing was opened at a local hospital, a special wing devoted to the deviant: Ward 15 was open for business. So Sioux City police officers raided men's rooms and resorted to the usual trickery of interrogating the frightened with veiled threats and subtle promises of hope. Lists were created, and kept. The different were targeted and some two dozen or more men were taken to a psychiatric facility and held for months while the mental health professionals tried to figure out why the men were there and what to do with them.

Neil Miller's *Sex-Crime Panic: A Journey To The Paranoid Heart of the 1950s* tells the tale with elegant and compelling prose. Although the book was written in 2002, it bears reading today. We are no less prone to the sort of moral panic that yields bad law now than folks were in the 1950s. We still resort to undiscriminating fear when confronted with a sex crime. All that has changed is the name of the victims.

"Despite their good intentions, sexual psychopath laws invariably took a catch-all approach to sex offenders. The intended targets may have been rapists and murderers, but in almost every state with a sexual psychopath law, little or no distinction was made between nonviolent and violent offenses, between consensual and nonconsensual behavior, or between harmless 'sexual deviates' and dangerous sex criminals," Miller writes of the 1950s.

We struggle with the same sense of panic today. Hence Megan's Law, requiring registration of an ever-expanding class of so-called sex offenders, ranging from Romeo and Juliet couplings, to folks who urinate in public, to folks who look at the wrong sort of pictures. Paranoia runs deep in American culture; fear of the other reflects a deep current in mainstream of American life.

"Sex crime panics—and panics of all sorts—are very much in the American grain, from the Salem witch trials down to our own time.... Public fears and anxieties can lead to the enactment of bad laws, and laws enacted in an atmosphere of fear and anxiety can lead to even worse consequences," Miller writes, with an eye as much looking forward as to the tragic past in Sioux City.

There's something wrong when a society makes a celebrity of the surviving family of a crime victim. What's worse is taking a shocking crime and treating it as somehow reflecting the norm in deviance. Adam

Walsh's father is a celebrity, recognized for no accomplishment of his own save his very public grief and anger. And yet, Congress passed a law to extend sex offender registration because of the pressure Mr. Walsh brought to bear. What truly shocks and damages about the phenomenon is that there is not one shred of evidence to suggest Mr. Walsh's son was harmed by a sex offender. I wonder what a social historian will make of this pathology in the decades to come, and how many lives will be destroyed?

Our Supreme Court is not immune to this crazy hysteria, as it made clear in *United States v. Comstock*. The decision is chilling in that it asserts a broad federal police power foreign to historic conceptions of the role of the federal government. And we like sheep let this happen, because the government set its sights on sex offenders. Who is next, I wonder? Perhaps dissidents? Or tax protestors?

The federal government is supposed to have limited powers. That was the framers' intent. Those powers not expressly given to the federal government were retained either by the people or the individual states. A significant portion of our history has been a sustained struggle about where to draw the line distinguishing state and federal power.

The United States Supreme Court all but ignored that line in *Comstock*. It did so in a way that terrifies. Call in it the therapeutic state writ large.

The case involved the decision of the federal government to detain five prisoners after they had served their criminal sentences. The men were all convicted sex offenders. Because the government believed that the men were mentally ill and still posed a danger to reoffend, they moved to commit them civilly, under a federal statute. Three of the men were convicted of possession of child pornography, one was convicted of illegal contact with a minor, the fifth was convicted of aggravated sexual assault of a minor.

Under the federal civil commitment statute, the men could be detained after serving their sentences if the government showed, by clear and convincing evidence, that the men had either engaged in, or attempted to engage in, sexually violent conduct or child molestation, or suffered from a serious mental illness, abnormality or disorder. If a prisoner falls into either of these two classes and is deemed to be sexually dangerous to others or would have serious difficulty in refraining from sexually violent conduct or child molestation, he can be detained after he has served his term of imprisonment. A potential detainee has a right to a hearing, counsel, and the right to put on evidence. But a detainee has no right to a jury. This loss of liberty is regarded as civil rather than criminal in character. Whether a person is to remain detained can be reviewed every six months on demand of the detainee. Listen carefully: Indefinite detention based on the government's assessment of a risk to public safety. All this without the safeguard of jury review.

The government has the power to retain a person indefinitely and the detained man has no right to a jury trial. This is the sort of decision that should have people protesting in the street. But the decision was met with silence because those locked up are feared.

The Court justifies this sweeping new federal power as little more than business as usual. This power is simply a power necessary and proper under Art. I, Section 8 of the federal Constitution.

What shocks is that the Court refuses even to make passing reference to the Ninth Amendment of the Constitution. That amendment, the forgotten child of the federal Constitution, reads as follows: "The enumeration in the Constitution, of certain rights, shall not be construed to deny or disparage others retained by the people." The Court has never, in more than two hundred years of jurisprudence, paid more than lip service to those rights retained by the people. Did anyone consult we the people about giving the federal government the right to hold a person indefinitely without so much as a jury trial for looking at dirty pictures?

This decision expands federal power in significant ways. First, it applies a statute that was no doubt intended to hold violent felons to those accused of merely looking at pictures. Assuming that this is a disorder, is it really a crime involving sexual violence to a child or child molestation? On this broad application of the statute, the federal government would be justified in seeking unlimited detention of anyone who looked at a prohibited image of a child.

Students of constitutional law are familiar with the enumerated powers doctrine. It is said that the federal government is one of limited powers. To the states, the theory goes, belong the police powers, that authority governing the health, education and welfare of a citizenry.

Granting the federal government what amounts to an expanded police power in a climate of moral panic is chilling. The federal government does on occasion prosecute men federal prosecutors believe have already been convicted in the state courts, but have been dealt with too leniently by the states. In one Connecticut case, a state court gave a defendant a suspended sentence, involving no term of imprisonment, for the crime of possessing child pornography. Outraged federal prosecutors brought separate charges for the same offense, securing a four-year prison term. This is no violation of double jeopardy, lawyers know, as different sovereigns can see things differently, but it is still shocking.

The federal government has customarily served as a counterweight when the states succumb to craziness. In *Comstock*, the Court became the chief cheerleader for what can easily amount to state-sponsored craziness.

The Court merely reflects the wholesale craziness of our sexophrenia. When it comes to claims of child sex, we've abandoned reason. Consider the following claim: the vast majority of those accused of possessing child pornography have actually abused children. This is simple silliness. Yet it is the sort of message our tax dollars send when we subsidize such groups as the National Center for Missing and Exploited Children.

Ernie Allen, president of NCMEC, recently told The New York Times: "Real children are harmed in the production of these images and these same children are harmed every time these images are downloaded and viewed." He presumably gets paid a decent sum for uttering this specious idiocy.

Almost every single one of the men I have represented in criminal cases arising from the possession of child pornography is guilty of bad judgment or simple curiosity. Some suffer psychological maladies. In the dozens of sex offense cases I've handled, I have yet to see any causal link between looking at pictures and molesting actual children.

If you have not seen the film *Reefer Madness*, check it out. It's a 1936 propaganda film about the dangers of smoking marijuana. Marijuana, you see, is the gateway drug of the masses. Start with weed, and end up choking on far more serious drugs. The descent to madness starts with but a single puff. The line between fact and fear is easily blurred.

The National Center for Missing and Exploited Children is one of the primary culprits blurring the line between fact and fancy. Yes, real children, when they are used to produce a film or photograph, are harmed. The production of child pornography misuses children and should be a crime. But the children are not harmed anew when, in some dank and musty basement thousands of miles away, a shame-faced man sneaks a peak at the images. To suggest otherwise is to live in a fool's paradise.

But opposing sex offenses is a cheap and easy way to score points politically. So every time lawmakers want to feel good about something, they slap a new law, a new restriction, a new mandatory minimum sentence on those accused of sex crimes. Child sex is the new crack cocaine. We want to stamp it out, so we criminalize it. Just when it begins to dawn on folks that the war on drugs really doesn't work, we start a new moral crusade. What is it about our political culture that requires always that there be a villain, some other that we can attack to displace all that makes us uneasy?

Few judges have the courage to call this madness out and to refuse to go along with the charade we call justice. It is not justice to put a man in prison for looking at pictures. It is not justice to lock away a young man for flirting with a police officer pretending to be a 14-year-old runway model in heat. Justice requires individual assessments of harm and risk. Most judges, however, approach the task of sentencing like assembly-line workers. Along comes a defendant, the judge looks at the instruction manual produced by lawmakers, and then the judge clips the defendant so that he fits the image the cookie cutter yields. This sort of judging brings the judiciary into disrepute.

That's why I love Jack B. Weinstein, an 88-year-old federal judge in Brooklyn. Weinstein's been on the bench for 43 years. When he sees a law that is offensive to justice, he refuses to enforce it. Oh, that

President Barack Obama were to find a few more Weinsteins to put on the bench. Instead, we get bloodless automatons.

Weinstein has refused to impose mandatory minimum sentences when the sentence did not fit the defendant, as he did in the case of Pietro Polizzi, a New York man who collected more than 5,000 prohibited pictures. Sure, Polizzi violated the law, but he is also married and a father of five children. Judge Weinstein refused to throw him in prison for many years, recognizing the man made what amounts to a libidinal mistake, but is not a monster.

We need more Jack Weinsteins on the bench. Things are spiraling out of control in child pornography cases. In 2009, there were more than 1,600 federal prosecutions; the previous year there were fewer than 100. The average prison sentence in a federal child pornography case is 91 months; a decade ago, the average was 21 months. We're putting more people in jail for longer periods as a result of hysteria. Why don't we give judges power to stop the madness when they see it?

CHAPTER 11

HOW TO REFORM SEXOPHRENIC LAWS

The single most important criminal justice reform within reach in each statehouse is the elimination of mandatory minimum prison sentences and consequences. The ends of justice require it. Sound economics counsel it. Only anger and fear stand in the way of meaningful reform. Consider the craziness our courts require regarding statutory rape, sexual contact between two willing participants where one of the parties is deemed too young as a matter of law to give consent.

Law students are taught, and judges still pretend, that a judgment of guilty and a criminal sentence should accomplish four purposes: deterrence of the individual who committed the crime, deterrence of others who might commit a similar crime, rehabilitation of the guilty, and retribution. We teach that to practitioners of the law, but not to lawmakers. They are presumed to know these things.

Lawmakers need re-education about the purposes of the criminal justice system. This is necessary because lawmakers increasingly resort to a one-size-fits-all mindset when it comes to mandating penalties for crimes. The fact of the matter is that offenders, and that includes sex offenders, are rarely identical. Justice requires a measured and calibrated response to the nature of the offense and the character of the offender.

I have sat in judge's chambers and listened to private agonizing by both the judge and the prosecution. A young man who confesses to a

Romeo and Juliet crime, falling in love with a young girl below the age of consent, but consenting nonetheless to sexual contact, must be sent to prison, convicted of a felony, be required to register as a sex offender, and undergo treatment for sexual misconduct as a consequence of his inevitable probation. These four horsemen appear at the doorstep to the judge's chambers, but each horseman smirks: they know that some of the men and a few of the women in the room are guilty of doing just what the young man did, they just weren't caught. So the judge does his job, accepts the defendant's guilty plea, and sends him to prison. It is as inevitable as an assembly line.

A criminal offense, and the consequences of committing the offense, including prison and registration as a sex offender, are mandated by lawmakers. Yet these lawmakers are never required to meet the men and women sentenced, or to make any assessment of what risk, if any, they pose to society. In a legislative chamber, lawmakers strike out in the name of decency and innocence. Protecting children is their battle cry. Who would fail to rally to such a standard? The trouble is that these rallying cries often deafen those who want to listen to what justice requires. Lawmakers never see the consequences of their laws at work in a courtroom.

The crime of statutory rape has a history. Prior to the industrial revolution, the age of consent was low in many states, reaching to 10 years of age in some states. It was assumed that parents and local communities could police the conduct of young people learning to cope with newly emergent hormones. When young women began to flock to cities from their farms in search of factory work, young women were unsupervised in urban centers. The Women's Christian Temperance Union sponsored legislation increasing the age of consent to 16 and 18 years old. This reform swept the states in the 1880s, and its product remains the law today.

What prompted the law was not a conclusion that love is a crime, but a fear familiar to current efforts to expand the sex offender registry at every chance: stranger danger. If young women were far from home, any predator could take advantage of them. The law was never intended to crush those young men and women who fell in love before lawmakers thought they should. Romeo ought not to be required to register as a sex offender.

I am not writing in favor of decriminalizing sex offenses. These crimes cut to the very core of a person's sense of self-worth and dignity. When actual crimes occur, they should be punished. But I am proposing that mandatory minimum sentences be eliminated so that judges can decide what the appropriate punishment and consequences should be.

How should sentencing of sex offenders take place? We should replace mandatory minimum sentences with rebuttable presumptions.

A rebuttable presumption is a target. Lawmakers can say that for a given offense, a mandatory term of imprisonment of, let's say, one year is presumed reasonable. If a party facing such punishment thinks the prison term should be less than that, he and his lawyer would be free to rebut the presumption by giving the judge reasons to impose a lesser sentence. Thus, in the case of a Romeo and Juliet law, society could maintain its judgment that sex below a certain age is unwise and prohibited, but realize that to every rule there are exceptions.

Reform advocates in each state and on the federal level should target statutes requiring mandatory prison time and registration for extinction. Each time you read the word "shall" in a statute, a term of art eliminating judicial choice, rewrite the law to state "should, unless given reasons to do otherwise." Judges will often do the right thing if lawmakers let them. We need to persuade legislators to give judges the freedom to make judgments.

We should also revisit the privileged place we are giving to the testimony of children.

Lawyers representing folks accused of sex offenses know the power of mere words. An accusation standing alone, without corroboration, can condemn a person whether they have committed a crime or not. Often these words come from children. And once a child makes a claim, the state abandons its critical apparatus and works to foster an environment in which accusations are treated as "disclosures." We give tremendous power to children by treating them as oracles of shameful truths.

There will come a time in which our incredulity about the words of children will look as troubling as the manner in which we treated accused witches in Salem, Massachusetts. In 1692, 19 men and women and two dogs were convicted and executed for consorting with the Devil. These deaths were the product of the words of children who claimed to have been seduced by a Satan-worshipping household servant named Tituba.

Arthur Miller wrote a play about the trials in 1953, *The Crucible.* He viewed the Salem trials as a prism through which the activities of the House Un-American Activities Committee's prosecution of Americans for disloyalty could be viewed. What gives so much power to mere accusation? Why are we sometimes ripe for an hysteria that is so easily seen to be false in a calmer moment?

I wish Miller were writing now. I'd like to see what he would make of the moral panic present in our courts whenever the state chooses to adopt the words of a child as a truth worth fighting for. We do not permit children to make contracts, and regard them as incapable in most of life's serious affairs. But yet, if the state chooses to take the uncorroborated claim of a child as truth, to treat it as a disclosure based upon which it can and should deprive a man or woman of liberty, then a defendant is left often as helpless to combat the claims as were the true victims at Salem.

I re-read *The Crucible* recently to prepare for a civil trial in which a client sued the mother of a child who made extravagant claims. The mother defended by saying that it was her job to believe and support her child. I asked the jury to conclude that it was also the mother's job to behave responsibly, and to provide guidance to her child. Treating children as oracles is always dangerous. We won, proving defamation and intentional infliction of emotional distress, known in some states as outrage. It was an encouraging verdict.

I read the following words from *The Crucible* to the jury during my opening statement and closing argument. "Is the accuser always holy now? Were they born this morning as clean as God's fingers? I'll tell you what's walking Salem—vengeance is walking Salem. We are what we always were in Salem, but now the little crazy children are jangling the keys of the kingdom, and common vengeance writes the law."

Children do not deserve privileged status in our courts. Perhaps it is time to reinvigorate the Mosaic "two witness" rule, once required in homicide cases, and apply it to child sex cases. In those cases in which liberty hangs solely on the word of a child, and in which there is no other witness or any physical proof of harm, it should simply be too risky to prosecute. Massachusetts learned that the hard way in Salem; why do we need to learn the lesson all over again?

We used to permit juries to nullify the law when they thought it was wrong. In the early twentieth century, the Supreme Court forbade the practice in the federal courts; few states permit it. We need to rethink that rule. Shouldn't juries have a say in what is done in their name? Judge Weinstein plans to do what trial lawyers regard as the unthinkable in a child pornography trial: he is going to tell the jury what penalty the defendant faces if convicted. That practice almost never occurs. We make infants of jurors all the time, telling them lies and half-truths, and then declaring we have done justice. God bless Jack Weinstein for refusing to play charades with the lives of others.

We need, I say again, more Jack Weinsteins on the bench. At least, I think we do. We've a few too many fools in Congress, and far too many crusading for the right thing but using the wrong means.

Those of us who earn our living on the front lines of the criminal justice system are often too shell-shocked to recognize larger trends. But when things go beyond a mere trend, and take the form and shape of a tsunami, everyone notices. Allegations of sexual misconduct with minors are the latest tidal wave to inundate the courts.

There was a time when it seemed as if every other call for representation was from some soul caught within the web of a federal indictment for conspiring to sell crack cocaine. Here's how the game was played: The feds would target a suspected dealer. They'd watch him, record his phone conversations, and then, after several weeks, sweep in and arrest every person who as much as touched a rock of crack. Those at the periphery of the action were expected to plead guilty and get favorable terms in exchange for fingering those at the center of the conspiracy.

These cases became an art form, with predictable acts, plots and characters. (Client: "We never talked about the coke on the phone." Lawyer: "Yes, I know you talked about shrimp. But tell me, what have you to corroborate that you were really in the business of selling seafood?") Once you've seen a couple dozen of these, you've pretty well seen them all.

Today new melodramas are unfolding. They all involve child sex claims. People are accused of either looking at child pornography online, enticing a purported minor online to have sex, or groping a niece or daughter of a friend. Law enforcement has got its game down pretty well now, so expect more and more of these cases to be brought until, for reasons as yet unforeseen, some new fashion sweeps lawmen off their feet.

I'm not the only lawyer to observe this trend. I live in a tiny jurisdiction, and cover courthouses throughout my state. Lawyers gossip about what they are doing. Many lawyers are stunned by the sudden volume in these cases. Sex, I say, is the new crack.

I doubt seriously that some new wave of lechery has overtaken our society. In terms of the actual contact between adults and minors, I suspect things are pretty much the way they have always been. Sometimes the wrong things go bump in the night. We no longer overlook these transgressions: today we seek long periods of incarceration in the effort to banish untoward desire.

But what has changed is the ubiquity of images on the Internet. I represent plenty of young men who took their libido for a walk online. Some of them got curious about things they might never try. They looked at pictures of forbidden acts. Now the state and federal government want them to go to prison. It seems like a waste of life and human potential.

Other young men dabble at sex online. The forms this lust takes are sadly common. If I hear about another guy in his twenties promising an undercover cop posing as a 14-year-old girl that he will teach her to give oral sex like a porn star, I'll sigh a deep groan of despair. I fear that Dante's vision of Hell is far more interesting than the warp and woof of our contemporary sins. Lust is ugly; we bend in only so many grotesque ways.

But here is what I worry about: as law enforcement perfects the craft of prosecuting these cases, the standard for when to prosecute will get lower and lower. I represented a young man accused of possessing four images of child pornography on his computer. This calls for prison. If there were only three images, he'd go free. So we fight now about whether he actually looked at all four images, and whether that matters. Were lawmakers thinking when they passed laws calling for mandatory prison time?

Or consider a recent statute in Connecticut, aggravated sexual assault in the first degree. Touch two or more children under the age of 13 in an improper manner, and you look a twenty-five year mandatory sentence dead in the eye. That's the same penalty as required for manslaughter with a firearm. The real import of a statute like this is to frighten defendants into a guilty plea: anything to avoid the risk of trial, whether they are guilty or not.

It is far too easy for lawmakers to pass legislation with draconian sentences from within the antiseptic chambers of a legislative assembly. Who, after all, wants to appear to go easy on those who abuse children? But not all forms of abuse are identical, and neither are all defendants. Sometimes a mistake is just a mistake, and the harm that comes of making it a crime dwarfs all justice. I wish that lawmakers were required to go to court to see their handiwork.

I wish that each lawmaker were required to spend a few months behind bars to get a sense of what it is to live isolated and afraid. Is it too much to ask those who make the product to test drive what they are producing? Do lawmakers have any idea what follows from conviction of a sex crime? How many of them are secretly guilty of the conduct they criminalize?

It was reassuring to see the United States Supreme Court chip away at the collateral consequences doctrine in *Padilla v. Kentucky*. By ruling that criminal defense counsel have an affirmative obligation to advise their clients about the immigration consequences of a plea, the Court moved one step closer to reality. Let's hope it is not the last step.

Padilla entered a guilty plea in a Kentucky court. His lawyer told him not to worry about the immigration consequences of the plea. Padilla had, after all, been in the United States for 40 years although he was not a citizen. So Padilla pleaded guilty. And deportation proceedings promptly began. He was on a one-way ticket out of the land of the free.

Our courts sidestep justice all the time by regarding the foreseeable consequences of a criminal conviction as merely incidental. Thus, in the case of a sex offender, courts permit convictions to stand when lawyers fail to make adequate warnings about all sorts of things, including the demeaning and often standardless manner in which so-called sex offender treatment is administered.

Does *Padilla* offer hope that the courts will take a broader view of the punishing collateral consequences of a guilty plea to a sex offense?

Anyone accused of a sex offense really faces four harms. Good lawyering requires advising a client about them all, and then doing what can be done to minimize the harm to the client arising from each of these harms.

The first two harms are obvious: the disabling effect of a felony conviction and imprisonment. These are the classic consequences of a conviction that all lawyers know and understand, although, I suspect, there may be some confusion regarding mandatory minimum sentences as these sentences change with legislative tastes.

The requirement to register on a sex offender registry and the need to participate in sex offender treatment as a condition of any probation are a direct and proximate consequence of a plea in most states. In other words, utter the word "guilty" and these consequences flow as irrevocably as, well, immigration problems.

If there is now a Sixth Amendment requirement to advise defendants of the immigration consequences of a plea, it follows that rights to due process and equal protection, and against cruel and unusual punishment, ought to be enforced in some meaningful way as to the consequences of a plea. It simply isn't good enough to permit courts to pass off miscarriages of justice arising from sex offender pleas as merely incidental consequences of a guilty plea.

Padilla v. Kentucky is important not just for the protection it offers to immigrants accused of crimes. It is important also as a new tool that just might help to mitigate the gratuitous harm done to those convicted of sex offenses. In the current climate of moral panic, we are failing to distinguish minor offenders from serial rapists. The result is a criminal justice system dealing out draconian consequences without meaningful review. *Padilla* offers the hope of change.

CHAPTER 12

LIAR, LIAR, ROBE ON FIRE

If you doubt that money matters in the administration of justice in our courts, consider the following: I have more access to information if I am defending an insurance company's stake in an automobile accident than I do in defending a man accused of murder. When it comes to the adversarial system of justice, money counts a whole lot more than liberty.

The civil courts permit parties to raise claims seeking money damages. Juries are told that they can award money damages to make a plaintiff whole insofar as money can do so. Money is a substitute for justice.

Thus, if you damage my car in a simple rear-end collision, I can present the bills to repair my car to a jury and ask for relief. So too with medical expenses. But what are we to do with pain and suffering? What is the value of a stiff neck, or of emotional distress? How are these things to be valued?

I have a confession to make: there is little more thrilling than to argue an intangible injury to a jury. But the thrill has less to do with doing justice than it has to do with the sort of rush one gets at a casino. You pull justice's lever, and see what comes tumbling out of the deliberation room.

I winced as I wrote this because it is too candid a truth. I may well see one of the readers of this book on a jury sometime. When I stand before the jury to ask for damages, I want that jury to believe that the numbers reflect some larger reality, some sense of justice that is at best measurable, if not completely objective. But there is no such thing as a scale of justice when it comes to intangible injury. All that we have to measure such damages is the good sense of a jury.

Whatever shortcomings I may have for being honest about the system, I am unwilling to lie about it. The big liars in the civil justice system are the insurance defense lawyers. These men and women serve two masters. Sitting beside them at trial is the individual defendant, a person accused of engaging in some sort of behavior the law does not permit. We call personal injury claims tort claims, deriving their name from a Latin term meaning "twisted."

But what is more twisted than presenting the insured to a jury and pretending that this hapless defendant is on the hook not just for damages, but for the legal fees necessary to try the case? The fact is that in most cases, a defendant is fully insured against a bad outcome. They are insured, and the jury never knows this. Indeed, whisper a word of this secret truth within earshot of the jury and watch a judge's blood pressure rise.

Keeping this information secret serves a laudable enough goal. We fear that juries aware of the presence of insurance will award too much money. Hence, we keep the focus on the individual and often hapless defendant. This assures that an award of damages will not be influenced by passion, prejudice or sympathy – the fateful troika of factors that are to be guarded against in all trials. But let's spend a moment deconstructing this logic.

Judges often say that a properly instructed jury is presumed to follow the law. In other words, if you tell people of good will what to do, they will do it. Absent some compelling evidence to the contrary, a presumption carries the day. Think of a presumption as the default setting on an electronic device. Unless something overrides this setting, it will govern.

We tell juries in virtually every civil case that they are not to be governed by passion, sympathy or prejudice. They are presumed to follow this rule of law. And then we pretend that the defendant is the modest person without means sitting humbly beside his or her lawyer. What became of the presumption that the jurors will follow the law? Is it all right to lie to juries if the lies have a tendency to depress the value of a verdict?

If you think I am over-reacting, consider the following: judges set aside verdicts all the time. The process is known as remittitur. A jury makes an award. It is told that it is the conscience of the community. But after the jury goes home, the defendant is free to ask the judge to reduce an award if the defendant thinks it is too high. Even when this happens, the courts pretend that there are no insurance companies underwriting the charade.

Many years ago, I won a verdict that shocked many observers; it even landed me as a guest on several national television shows, including the O'Reilly Factor. My client was Kevin King. He was a convicted killer against whom the state had sought the death penalty. A jury decided against death, however. So he was sentenced to life without possibility of parole.

King's crime was horrifying. He had beaten a young girlfriend to death as she babysat her toddler sister one Christmas season. He was represented in the criminal trial by the state's public defenders.

Shortly after the verdict, one of the public defenders called me and asked me if I would represent King. According to the public defender,

King had recently turned up in court bruised and bloodied. I was told that prison officials had beaten him up. I agreed instantly to take the case. The truth about this case was far more bizarre that I could have imagined when I agreed to be his lawyer.

During his criminal trial, King was held in a low-security jail near the courthouse. After his sentence was imposed, he would be moved to the state's supermax prison. If he wanted ever to escape, his best hope was to do so before he was transferred.

He planned an escape that required him to don the uniform of a guard and walk out the door. He studied his jailers, listening carefully to their conversations as they discussed what kinds of cars they drove. One night he put his plan into action. He lured a guard into his cell, and ordered her to take her uniform off. When she resisted him, he stabbed her in the chest with a shank, a homemade knife. He then tied the guard to his bed, gagged her, put her uniform on, and proceeded to walk out the door. He almost made it to freedom, her car keys in his pocket. But he was spotted at one of the final checkpoints. As alarms sounded, he turned to run, the shank in his hand.

At the end of a long corridor, he ran out of options. He faced a wall. Guards came running up behind him. He dropped to his knees, and placed his hands in front of him as he was forced to the ground. He tried to hide the shank in his hand from the guards, and managed to fall on it, an ice-pick like projectile digging deep into his chest near his heart. He felt certain that he would die. In fact, I suspect he more or less hoped he would.

The guards raised him to his feet and then took him to a holding cell. As they did, they learned of the assault of their fellow guard. The enraged guards struck King with their fists and kicked him, slamming him into open cell doors and walls every chance they could find. They later explained his modest bruises and injuries as resulting from their struggle to subdue a resisting inmate.

Of course, they did not know about the shank in King's chest. He was not going to resist. He was afraid to move and was doing all that he could to avoid further violence.

We tried the case before a jury in the Hartford federal court. It was a brief trial. The two lawyers on the other side were openly contemptuous of King, and why shouldn't they be? It was bad enough to have murdered a teenager. Now the man had attacked a correctional officer, too. What's more, he had the audacity to ask a jury for money damages.

I did not ask the jury for a specific sum in that case. I merely argued the obvious. Not one of us is the sum of our worst moments. All men and women are entitled to the equal protection of the law. The guards' decision to assault King and take the law into their own hands merely made them into a lawless gang, no better than the men they are to protect us against. I asked for money damages sufficient to compensate King for a fractured orbital socket and bruises; I also asked for punitive damages in an amount sufficient to tell prison officials that lawlessness would not be tolerated in our name behind prison walls.

The jury listened. It took its role as the conscience of the community seriously by awarding King $75,000 for the damages he suffered. But what was truly amazing in this case was the decision to award punitive damages against each of the two defendants we could identify: the jury awarded punitive damages of one million dollars against each man. The total verdict was almost $2.1 million.

The defendants attacked the verdict as too high, despite the fact that the defendants had offered no evidence that they were responsible for paying them. Indeed, as is the case in almost every verdict involving damages against a state official for violating a citizen's civil rights, the state was paying the damages. In other words, the state agreed to provide insurance to its employees, paying their damages when a jury concluded the employees have violated the constitutional rights of another citizen. In this case, the jury had concluded that the defendants violated King's right to be free from cruel and unusual punishment.

The trial judge agreed but reduced the verdict to a total of $350,000. The state took an appeal to the United States Court of Appeals for the Second Circuit, complaining that even that sum was too high. The appeals court left the verdict at $350,000 and, in the end, the state paid the money.

Did Mr. King ever see any of that money? Not really. My firm was entitled to an award of attorney's fees. We were given 40 percent of the total. The state seized the balance to pay for the cost of incarceration. In the end, we gave Mr. King a gift for his prison commissary account. It was a sloppy piece of justice.

Was the jury ever told that its role as conscience of the community was subject to judicial review? No, the judge made sweet, deceptive love to the folks assembled to decide the case. He made them feel as if they had the ability to speak harsh words to those in authority. The only way they will ever learn about what happened to their work is if they happen to stumble upon a report of the case. That's unlikely. Most jurors lead busy lives. I doubt many follow what becomes of their handiwork once a case ends.

The first case I ever won for money damages was against a couple of Connecticut state troopers who gave an arrestee a gratuitous kick in the groin after handcuffing him. My client, the arrestee, was not happy about being arrested. He was giving the officers a piece of his mind. It is no crime to tell an officer he is wrong. Although you can breach the peace of a fellow citizen by acts of mere speech, you cannot breach the peace of a police officer. That means officers are supposed to have thick enough skin to endure the tirades of those finding themselves on the receiving end of the law's long arm.

But some officers have short fuses. So when my client was seated on the ground with his hands cuffed behind him, one of the officers gave him a good boot in the balls. It hurt, my client testified, although it did not require medical attention.

A jury awarded my client $50,000 for the injury. The judge, a crusty old lifetime appointee to the federal bench, did not look too happy about it. As my client and I were walking out the courthouse door, a clerk came running up behind us. "Attorney Pattis, Attorney Pattis," she said. I turned. "The judge would like to see you."

I was led back into a room just off the courtroom in which we had tried the case. The judge was sitting in there with the lawyer who had represented the police officers.

"I think you should talk about settling this case now," the judge said.

"Settling?" I said. "We just won. I haven't even had a chance to stand on the courthouse steps and give my client a high-five for justice," I said. Modesty is not one of my gifts.

The judge was none too pleased. I don't recall much else about the conversation, but I have always been troubled by it. Had the jury found in favor of the police, would the judge have been as quick to summon my adversary in with a suggestion that he pay me money simply to avoid an appeal?

When I got back to my office, I was unbearable. I figured I was going to be the next F. Lee Bailey. A senior colleague talked me off the ceiling.

"When you win a verdict, the case is only halfway done," he said. "All a win does is enhance your bargaining position."

He was right, of course. The state attacked the verdict in a series of post-trial motions. We had additional court appearances. There was no jury in any of these proceedings. I am happy to report, however, that we got paid a year later. We were paid all $50,000 plus interest and modest attorney's fees. The judge simply could not find a way to tamper with the jury's verdict as the award was modest in sum.

In another case, a client was not so lucky.

Jim Lee was an off-duty police officer who went skiing with a friend one cold January night. When they got home sometime after midnight, there was nothing to eat at Jim's house. They decided to head out to a diner.

The roads were icy, and Jim had been drinking. As he rounded a corner, he rear-ended a parked car. The car's owner, a college security officer, came running out of his house a moment later; he was carrying a nightstick. Jim had crashed into another law-enforcement officer's car. Words were exchanged between the men and municipal police officers soon arrived. But before they got there, the car owner bludgeoned Jim with his nightstick. He later wrote in a police report that my client had attacked him, and that he had to use the nightstick in self-defense. The problem with that claim was that Jim's friend was standing right there and saw it all. The police report was a lie.

Jim was prosecuted for driving while intoxicated and assault on a police officer. The latter charge is a serious felony that could result in many years behind bars. My client was terrified when he saw what he had been charged with; that terror yielded to relief when the assault charge was dropped.

We filed a civil suit for malicious prosecution, claiming that the officer's report about being assaulted was bogus and made with malice, to get even with my client for damaging his car and mocking him. A jury awarded $1 in compensatory damages, no doubt expressing its disapproval that my client had been driving while impaired. But it also awarded $200,000 in punitive damages against the police officer. The jury was told by agreement of the lawyers that the municipal police department would pay for the punitive damages. In other words, the officer's ability to pay the damages was not an issue in the case.

Now clearly this was an unusual case, and odds are I will never see another one like it. Most often, civil defense lawyers fight to the death to prevent juries from learning who will pick up the tab in the event of a plaintiff's verdict. But the defendant's lawyer agreed to tell the jury this. She therefore could not complain about it later; in lawyerspeak, she waived any objections.

After the jury was sent home and had forgotten about the case, the lawyer for the police officer filed a motion asking the judge to reduce the punitive damages award. The trial judge declined to do so, in large measure because the defendant had agreed to let the jury know that the city's deep pockets stood behind the man who had abused my client. For once, a jury learned the truth: municipalities often insure police officers against the consequences of misconduct.

The defendant then filed an appeal in the United States Court of Appeals for the Second Circuit.

There are three levels of federal courts. Cases are initially decided in the District Court. There are 94 districts in the United States. My state, Connecticut, is small enough to be composed of but one district. Larger states, such as New York, have several districts. Once a case is decided in the district courts, the parties can take an appeal. The federal appellate courts are divided into 11 different circuits. Sitting atop the pyramid of the federal courts is the United States Supreme Court.

Connecticut, New York and Vermont all are part of the Second Circuit. The courthouse is located in Foley Square in Manhattan, not far from where the World Trade Center once stood. I've argued dozens of cases in the Second Circuit, and each case is a thrill. Some of the nation's finest legal minds have sat on that court. I am particularly moved by the sight of a bust of Learned Hand, a courageous lion of an intellect. Each time I enter the courtroom and see it, I am at once inspired, if only for a moment, by a sense of humility. The ghosts of some of the law's giants lurk in the courtroom: I tread warily, lest I awaken them. Typically, each case is heard by a three-judge panel. Both sides are given a very brief period of time in which to argue their case.

I was not concerned about Mr. Lee's case. A jury had decided the defendant acted with malice. That decision would hold. Although the defendant still sought a reduction in the amount of damages awarded against him, I was confident I could win that issue, too. After all, the city attorney defending the officer had waived the issue, right?

The Second Circuit stunned me, and taught me a lesson I am sorry to have learned over and over again: a police officer's best friend is more often than not wearing a black robe and swinging a gavel. The panel decided that $200,000 was an excessive sum. Police officers just don't make that kind of money. The court did something lawyers are taught never to do: it went outside the record to invent facts that were neither before the jury and were, in any case, irrelevant, given the concessions that the defense counsel had made before the jury. It was a lawless result; a result of the sort of judicial activism that conservatives decry, although, in this case, no pundits cried out in rage. When the court bends the rules to favor the state, there is very often little or no outrage from the public at large. I just don't get it. Don't the courts belong to the people?

After a couple of years of litigation, Mr. Lee collected a sum of $75,000, the number three judges plucked from thin air and decided was money enough to punish a cop who would not have to pay a dime in damages. The jury was never informed.

These anecdotal cases about how judges treat cases against a police officer help to prove a point: we get the government we deserve. When judges go out of their way to make the world safe for police misconduct, we should not be surprised to see stories about officers misusing Tasers, mishandling pregnant women, and generally behaving as if we are lucky they get up and strap on their holster in the morning. It sometimes feels as if the old Christian hymn "Trust and Obey" is becoming the new national anthem.

CHAPTER 13

JAILING THE ILL

Consider the Connecticut case of *State v. Connor*. Mr. Connor was suffering, at a minimum, from an achy-breaky heart and had unresolved issues with his ex-wife. So he did the only thing reasonable under the circumstances. He is alleged to have kidnapped her and taken her for something other than a joy ride. When he stopped at a gas station, she escaped the car. He was charged with a series of felonies, including violation of probation.

Mr. Connor was unhappy with his public defender, a man named M. Fred DeCaprio. (DeCaprio is, for my money, one of the state's top defense lawyers; if I am ever charged with a felony, I hope I am broke at the time. I want DeCaprio!) DeCaprio raised questions about whether the client was all there mentally. But the trial court simply appointed a new public defender. When new issues arose with that lawyer, the court finally ordered a competency hearing. Under Connecticut law, a defendant is incompetent if he unable to understand the proceedings or to assist in his own defense.

The evaluators were unable to determine whether Connor was competent since he refused to cooperate with them. After a series of court appearances at which, among other things, the issue of whether Connor was a malingerer was addressed, the court declared him incompetent and he was remanded to a psychiatric hospital. While there, he was still uncooperative with examiners, and he was eventually found competent by another judge. The court found that Connor was a malingerer and that he was capable of standing trial.

Are you confused yet? When the case reached trial before yet another judge, Connor again complained about his lawyer. He then demanded the right to represent himself. After extensive questioning by the court, he was granted the right to self-representation and was almost inevitably convicted.

The state of the law at the time of trial was governed by the federal case of *US v. Godinez*, which held that the legal standard for waiving the Sixth Amendment right to counsel was identical to that for determining competency. But *Godinez* merely grazed the real issue, missing the mark by a nuanced mile: in *Godinez*, the defendant waived his right to counsel and then plead guilty. Would he have been competent to conduct a trial?

The Supreme Court has made clear its view that mere competence to stand trial requires so minimal a mental state that it does not warrant the assumption that competence entails the ability to actually conduct a trial. Say what you want about trial lawyers, but it takes special skill to try a case: imagine playing chess on several dimensions, while tap-dancing, and all the while attempting to display calm amid chaos.

"[A] right of self-representation at trial will not affirm the dignity of a defendant who lacks the mental capacity to conduct his defense ... the spectacle that could well result from [the representation of the nominally competent] is at least as likely to prove humiliating as ennobling," the Court noted.

The states are free to confront as they see fit the stark reality that "a defendant, although minimally competent to stand trial, is not necessarily competent to represent himself at trial." In other words, just because you are nominally competent, it does not follow that you can conduct a trial. The result is a new doctrine in Connecticut, which, since the state's Supreme Court chose not to name it, I will: the doctrine of nominal competence.

Brace yourself. Here is the doctrine:

"[U]pon a finding that a mentally ill or mentally incapacitated defendant is competent to stand trial and to waive his right to counsel at that trial, the trial court must make another determination, that is, whether the defendant also is competent to conduct the trial proceedings without counsel." In other words, we will try the mentally ill as though they were not ill at all. The court acknowledges that a person can be mentally ill but competent.

I am not sure whether to applaud or to weep.

Why are we trying mentally ill or incapacitated people at all? Prison for the ill is a sick and perverted mockery. In the zero-sum universe of trial, the loser pays with his liberty, and prison is the last place I'd want a mentally ill loved one to go. Our Supreme Court's jurisprudence regarding the mentally ill has the look and feel of Jimmy Hendrix in a leper colony: all his brilliance will not yield music once he's lost the touch of his strings because his fingers are just stubs.

Most lawyers I know struggle with the mental health needs of at least some of their clients. We are not trained for this work, and generally make a mess of it. There are great fictions at work in the law. Perhaps the grandest of all is that of the reasonable person. The background assumption lurking beneath the surface of the common law is the notion that we are a community of reasonable minds. Folks bargaining in the law's shadow will reach the same conclusions, or, at the very least, will differ about conclusions along lines that all can identify and accept as rational.

But we are far from rational. Rage lurks in the shadows. So do anger, blind self-centeredness, paranoia and a host of other ghouls that may not rise to the level of out-and-out insanity, but which cloud the horizon. Cracking the sociopath's code, now that would be an accomplishment worthy of note. Imagine how much simpler life would be if we could turn away rage with a kind word, or, in the alternative, know how to discern anger which is appropriate to its place and circumstance from the infantile rage that bends everything toward itself?

Not enough has been written about mental health issues in the criminal law. A notable exception is *Crime, Punishment and Mental Illness: Law and the Behavioral Sciences in Conflict*, by Patricia and Steven Erickson. It is part of the Critical Issues in Crime and Society series published by Rutgers University Press in 2008.

In the criminal courts, voluntaristic assumptions about human behavior crash headlong into the emerging scientific understanding of the mind and its dysfunctions. The law cherishes its anachronistic commitment to punishment as a means of deterring those who choose to do wrong. Only those most severely ill are excused. But when a person is found not guilty by reason of insanity, he or she is warehoused nonetheless in an institution that has the look and feel of a prison. Our grand experiment with deinstitutionalization of the mentally ill has failed; we're now inclined to imprison a deviant rather than treat him. So much is obvious.

The grand crimes of the criminal courts merely illustrate truths we refuse to face in the civil courtroom: what fuels a good deal of litigation is the high octane energy that flows from minds bent and twisted beyond reason. The failures we tolerate in the criminal justice system are replayed a thousand-fold in the civil system, driving up litigation costs, clogging dockets and wearying a court staff not trained to play intermittent therapist.

I wonder why the tort reformers of the world have not focused on this issue. And I wonder why there is a dearth of literature on character disorders and the civil justice system. Perhaps because we fail where mental illness is most obvious, we simply despair of the more nuanced tragedies that take place daily in the civil court.

CHAPTER 14

TOO MANY LAWYERS: TIME TO REVISIT THE AMERICAN RULE

Most lawyers are not really honest about what they see day by day in their practices. They fear that if they told the truth, they'd have no more work. What most lawyers will acknowledge, privately, when only other fellow lawyers are around, is that there are simply too many of us. The result is that many lawyers are desperate for work.

And what do desperate lawyers do? They sue people. Why not? Access to the courts is inexpensive, and there is no downside. You might always hit a big verdict. And even if you lose, the so-called American Rule shields both lawyer and client from having to cover the costs of the winner. The American Rule has transformed the American civil justice system into the equivalent of a roulette wheel. Why not spin the wheel when the costs of doing so are low?

But there is another truth that lawyers are even more reluctant to utter, and that is the world is filled with angry people. Anger drives a good deal of the civil justice system. If you doubt it, ask the next plaintiff's lawyer you meet about the concept of client control. It's a notion untaught in law schools, but as real as the ink on a dollar bill.

Client control means the ability of a lawyer to get his or her client to follow the lawyer's recommendation. A civil dispute works in the following way: a person who thinks they are aggrieved visits a lawyer. The lawyer listens, and, armed with the minimal comprehension of the law acquired to pass the bar exam, the lawyer provides a "diagnosis." In other words, a set of legal doctrines are summoned that define whether the client has a cause of action. The lawyer then engages the client in a discussion about reasonable outcomes.

Consider a client who has been modestly injured in a car accident. The fault of the other driver is clear. So, too, is the fact that harm was caused. The client can obtain some small recovery. Many clients listen to their lawyers at this point. Some do not. Many of those who do not claim the lawyer does not understand the magnitude of the harm. They want millions for a hangnail. A lawyer who accepts such a client has no control over the litigation: the client's expectations are so high that the lawyer has no choice but to tilt at justice's windmill. One premier labor and employment firm in Connecticut provides a continuing legal education course to lawyers designed to help them identify just which clients' cases are worth the investment of time and money: lawyers are taught how to spot winning investments, and to turn away losers, most often by referring them to other lawyers, a practice I call "smurfing." Angry clients drive a significant portion of the plaintiff's market for legal services.

As luck would have it, the vagaries of the jury system make windmill tilting a profitable sport. I've from time to time "hit" enormous verdicts that I simply did not see coming. There are lawyers who specialize in angry clients. These folks will pay good money down for a chance at justice's roulette wheel.

I've learned to steer clear of blind anger. Indeed, I've learned to see limitless anger as a sin. As Henry Fairlie once noted in *The Seven Deadly Sins Today*: "[T]he love of justice is again and again turned into hatred of someone. Whenever love is turned into hatred, we know that sin has entered and wreaked its havoc." This sin may have moral causes, or it may be simple narcissism and no sin at all, but the fact remains that a lack of any sense of boundaries, in this case boundless rage, is an emotion at the core of much civil litigation.

I used to think of sin as an antiquated notion, somehow dependent on a set of transcendent rules made obsolete by the virtual absence of God. I now know better. I see sin in myself. I remain vigilant and struggle to keep in check the raw emotions and desires that are never too far below the surface of things. Anger, it turns out, is an easy sin. I hear it often on the phone: a caller all but shouts into the line that their rights have been violated. Will I take their case? Often, the rights are nothing more than desires unrecognized by law. Fairlie notes: "To present as rights what cannot in the end be secured as rights, as we all too often do today, is as sure a prescription for Wrath as any other that could be proposed."

The civil justice system is overloaded with anger and rage. Mind you, I am not saying that there is no room for the pursuit of justice in the courts, and that means there's room for righteous indignation. There are cases that should be brought, and relations that can be righted by law. But in too many cases, there is simply the raw hatred of a party seeking some sense of validation the law can never offer. The civil justice system has no mechanism for screening the meritorious from non-meritorious cases. And so long as there is a surfeit of lawyers, there will be an incentive for the legal profession to bring claims lacking in value. The American Rule makes sure this will happen.

But what happens to the party sued in a case driven by sinful anger? This party will most often win the litigation in the end. Experienced lawyers have a pretty good eye for risk in most cases. There are surprises, but those cases are outliers. Most often, cases are resolved more or less as expected by those with experience to know what they are seeing.

In cases driven by hatred, seething anger, or a need for validation unrelated to the merits of the actual claim, a defendant pays for his defense. And he pays dearly. And when he wins, the plaintiff and his or her lawyer walk away with impunity. It is simply wrong to permit this, and wasteful.

Defenders of the American Rule say that it provides all Americans with access to the courts, whether they have resources or not. I agree that it does, and I agree that it is a value that should be served. But I see no justice or fairness in requiring defendants, whether they be corporations or individuals, to pay unwarranted legal fees. Why shouldn't a loser be required to cover the winner's costs?

Here's my proposal: require all plaintiffs' lawyers to post bonds sufficient to cover the eventual winner's reasonable legal fees for all the cases they bring. This would protect the rights of all Americans to get justice in the courts. Plaintiffs would not be barred from bringing any claim they can persuade a lawyer to file. But defendants would also have the protection of recouping their fees when the roulette wheel comes up a loser for the plaintiff.

The proposal is not as far-fetched as it seems. Much like bondsmen, who post bonds for those released pending trial in a criminal case, a lawyer could be approved to float bonds up to the limit of the insurance policy he purchased to cover the bonds. A lawyer in this case would be free to take any case he wanted, and for which his client was willing to pay. The lawyer would be required, however, to pay the loser's costs from the bond posted.

This new regime could be flexibly applied. Make such a bond a rebuttable presumption in all civil cases. A judge would be free to relax the bond requirement for good cause—call it a prejudgment remedy for defendants.

Such a rule would have an additional benefit: once a lawyer was unable to secure insurance for additional bonds, he or she would have to decide whether to post his or her own assets as security. I suspect this rule would force a lot of lawyers to think twice before filing a frivolous writ.

I do not know how much money is spent in defense of civil suits each year. But I'll bet the sum is enormous, and I'll bet winning defendants often lose big even when they obtain a judgment in their favor. They lose big because the American Rule is, frankly, an invitation to gamble with other people's fortunes. That seems downright un-American to me.

CHAPTER 15

BUILDING BETTER LAWMAKERS

Term limits are a way of circulating elites in a political system. We fear that should folks serve in positions of power too long they'll lose touch with the broader currents pulsating in a society. Yet term limits impose a cost: experience matters. If we impose term limits, do we deprive ourselves of the leadership of those best able to manage our affairs? Doesn't it take time and wisdom to learn how to govern?

I have a proposal designed to improve the criminal justice system. No lawmaker should be able to seek re-election to a third term unless he or she agrees to serve six months in prison.

The benefits of such a system should be obvious to everyone.

Lawmakers churn out additions to the penal code annually. When they are not adding new offenses, they are extending the length of sentences for offenses already defined. A congressman or a state legislator has great power to set the terms and conditions under which increasing numbers of Americans live. Indeed, the penal code is now so vast and complex that we are almost all criminals at least part of the time. When everyone breaks the law, the rule of law breaks down as prosecutors acquire the discretion to pick and choose whom to punish.

Lawmakers tinker with the penal code without much comprehension of the real cost of what they are doing. Let's spread the pain a little,

I say. Let's make sure the good men and women so quick to throw the book at folks read the spines of those books.

The fact is that the American criminal justice system is savage. We imprison a greater percentage of our population than any other industrialized nation. And the sentences we impose for all manner of offenses are staggeringly long. We've transformed the penal system, some say, into a human waste management program: those folks we cannot integrate into society we isolate. Forget rehabilitation as a goal of imprisonment. Today the goal is to isolate and incapacitate. We boast of our unique qualities as a society without ever pausing to consider how we can tolerate the waste of so much human potential.

I've seen teenagers sentenced to 20 years for drug sales. A snap act of violence can yield 30, 40, 50 years or more stuffed in a concrete box. Do we really believe that these sentences serve any social utility? Aren't they really a hypocritical concession of failure?

I am confused, frankly. I watch the great rush to enact new and harsher laws against sex offenders, for example, and I wonder: how has the human race survived the ascent from ape to this, the most rational of all possible worlds? I don't recall as a young man learning my way in the world that I should be afraid of every stranger, that I should be wary of things going bump in the night if I sat on an uncle's lap, that desire was so unbounded that every embrace was a libidinal trap. We're in the midst of a semi-literate moral panic where we cannot make the world safe enough for children. We're so infatuated with this vision of safety that we're rushing to create a utopia. Unfortunately, as readers of political philosophy know, utopia means, literally, "no place."

What impulse leads lawmakers to sacrifice thousands of men and women to ideals that bear such faint correspondence to reality? Is it because it feels good to enact a new law? Or is it worse? Does every mob need a leader, someone to stoke hysteria when anxiety is unbounded? The past 100 years have seen great moral energy placed into prohibiting things: alcohol, Communists, drugs, wayward libido. But in each case, the law crashes against walls it cannot overcome. After a generation or so of social slaughter, lawmakers back off, regroup, and accept what they cannot change: that the mass of men really do lead lives of quiet desperation. I wonder whether the sin of Sloth, the inability to perceive some larger spiritual vision of a good, but flawed, society, has led us to become moral monsters forever chasing some caricature of the good.

So I say require lawmakers to live in the holes into which they consign so many Americans. It's not such an onerous suggestion, really. No one is forcing a lawmaker to pack his bags for a stay in the Hotel Despair. A lawmaker can walk away from power and its perquisites after a few terms. But if the hunger for power remains, then let power face the stark reality of what it can do to a man or woman: put the lawmaker away and deprive him of the liberty to hug his wife, kiss his child or dream the modest dreams that console his constituents.

Lawmakers fresh from a bid in a penitentiary will come to view a ten-year sentence as plenty long and sufficient to punish most crimes. And I doubt that many men and woman who have actually heard a prison door close behind them will be so quick to think that locking someone up actually accomplishes anything of value.

Almost every time I stand in the presence of a group of people to talk about sex offenses and accused sex offenders, I face the scorn of those assembled. Few crimes are as reviled. But when I stood recently in the auditorium of a church in Washington, D.C., and faced a friendly group of sex offender law reformers, I felt as though I was among dear friends. Imagine, a hundred or so folks looking upon me with approval as I bemoaned the face of defendants savagely ostracized from crimes of simple desire.

I was a guest of the second annual conference on reforming sex offender legislation sponsored by a group called, appropriately enough, Reform Sex Offender Legislation. It felt good. I know the sorrow they and their families have faced in the relentless and indiscriminate prosecution of these cases.

One thing is abundantly clear: our laws fail to discriminate between and among the various forms of sex offenses. There simply is a difference between a violent sexual offender and a young man who looked at a few pornographic images of children online or engaged in consensual sex with a young neighbor close in age. But the law requires a one-size-fits-all response to these offenses once a person is released from prison: requiring everyone to register as a sex offender is draconian. Do lawmakers ever pause to count the cost of such requirements? Law-enforcement resources are stretched to the breaking point by requiring the policing of so many Americans, most of whom are a threat to no one.

I said as much and more to an audience already persuaded. They've lived on the front lines of this war against over-criminalization and hysteria. At the end of my part of the presentation, someone asked what it would take to get a committee or group of lawyers together from around the country to serve as an intellectual catalyst for change. I told the speaker that I thought there was such support, although it might not yet have taken shape in the form of a formal committee. "You are closer than you think," I said. "You might just be the foot, and I might just be the ass." I am now on a legal committee associated with reforming sex offender legislation, although I am a reluctant participant.

I've never really trusted movement lawyers. The law is not philosophy. Individual clients come to me and I do not want to be encumbered by anything more than the very discrete and tangible interests of my client. No two clients are alike; each brings his or her own menu of issues to the table.

But I wonder, just now. I responded to the call to attend the event because I had seen one client after another decimated by the law's unfeeling and unthinking rigidity. I believe reform of sex offender laws is necessary. At this stage, I do not think that there is much the courts are willing and able to do. Most judges adopt a form of intellectual cowardice when things get tense: like junior officers in the Nuremberg dock, they plead that they were just following orders when they mete out justice with a sledgehammer. They blame legislators for the rules they are sometimes ashamed to enforce.

The front lines of reform will come in the state legislatures. That is where ordinary family members of those harmed by over-harsh laws can tell their stories to those with eyes open to the truth. We say of federalism that the states are laboratories of change. I believe this to be true. The federal government is no longer a progressive instrument for change: its scope is so broad it panders to the lowest common denominator. John Walsh is a hero on the national set; I for one find the 25-year national wake for his murdered son to be maudlin.

I reluctantly joined a committee of lawyers dedicated to changing the law. In confessing this, I acknowledge a certain moral and intellectual cop out. I left a promising academic career at its inception due to a certain epistemological weariness. If there were no larger truths, what was there to teach? The practice of law has liberated me, if not from the dark ghosts inhabiting a dark world, then at least from the paralysis and seeming nihilism that comes of a too-close familiarity with the leavings of what I sometimes feel is a spent Western intellectual heritage.

But the good people I saw in Washington, D.C., issued a challenge that echoes. What can be done, they asked, about the suffering their families and friends endure? Implicit in their question was a request for help. I've done some soul-searching. It's been perhaps too easy to sit on the sidelines and toss gratuitous scorn at visions of the good. Even if there is no certainty as to what goodness requires, that does not prohibit one from opposing unintended consequences resulting in something just this side of evil. I am not saying that sex offenders ought not to be punished; I am simply saying that not all offenses are alike.

There is a difference between violent rape and other forms of sexual misconduct, just as there is a difference between the inappropriate touching of a child and that of an adult. We all recognize that in the cold light of day. Perhaps that is why Al Gore was given a pass. Should he enjoy this privilege?

The former vice president apparently invited a masseuse up to a Portland, Oregon, hotel room in the Hotel Lucia in 2006. While there, he apparently made "unwanted sexual contact," needing more than a little kneading. The woman's lawyer contacted the police, but when she refused to be interviewed by law enforcement, the case was closed for lack of evidence. The woman's lawyer said she intended to sue Gore civilly.

It sounds an awful lot like a shakedown to me, although one really does question the wisdom of inviting a woman up to one's hotel room for some innocent flesh pressing. Is lust the national pastime?

Apparently, the civil suit did not turn out as well as the woman hoped it would, because in 2009 she finally turned up at the police station to make a complaint.

Multnomah County District Attorney Michael D. Schrunk told reporters the case was closed initially because "the woman was not willing to be interviewed by the Portland Police Bureau and did not want a criminal investigation to proceed." The case remains closed.

I'm not rooting for the prosecution of Al Gore. But I cannot help wondering whether he is getting a pass because of his status. I suspect there are many men in Portland labeled sex offenders for mere unwanted touching of another adult. Were their accusers required to come to court, summoned by material witness warrants? Why are these men labeled sex offenders? Is it because they lack Gore's status, wealth and power?

The testimony of a single witness, if believed, is enough to convict someone of a crime in the United States. In sex cases, that is sometimes all the state has, especially in child sex crimes. When a prosecutor decides in some cases that one witness is not enough, the public is right to wonder how such distinctions get drawn. Does a prosecutor have too much power when he or she can pick or choose whom to prosecute without review by any court or judicial officer?

Al Gore is lucky. He won't be charged with a sex crime. He won't be required to register as a sex offender. He won't be required to attend sex offender treatment where he will be required to admit to deviant desire or be sent to prison. But what about all the other guys who are destroyed by a criminal justice system that cannot distinguish a violent rape from an embarrassing mistake?

We need a better class of lawmakers to draw such obvious distinctions. Sending them to prison for a common sense refresher course is not so far-fetched as it seems.

CHAPTER 16

INTRODUCING GERRY DARROW

You might have missed the following news story. I will reprint it in its entirety, correcting only a few errors a kindly editor spotted.

Butner, North Carolina—President Barack Obama stood before a federal prison today and announced that he was nominating an unknown 42-year-old lawyer as the next justice of the Supreme Court, replacing retiring Justice John Paul Stevens.

"I promised hope when I asked for your trust during the last election. And you heard me. Together we transformed hope into a new and audacious reality. Today I redeem a part of my promise by naming a man who is no stranger to the suffering of ordinary Americans as the next Justice of the United States Supreme Court," the president said.

When the nominee stood to address the assembled press corps, there was an eerie silence. The man was on no short list of candidates. Indeed, he was a man few present had ever considered.

"I am flattered and humbled by this honor, Mr. President," Gerry Darrow said. "In all my years at the bar, I never dreamed that I would be considered for such a post. I've represented folks at the margins of society for so long, I had begun to think of myself as an outcast."

Thus began the improbable confirmation battle of a former plaintiffs' lawyer turned mid-life public defender.

Court watchers and legal academics were stunned by the nomination.

"Who?" said Laurence Tribe of the Harvard Law School. Even the Republican Party was stunned into momentary silence. "The man's an unknown, a cipher," said Senate Majority Leader Harry Reid. "We will, of course, have questions for him. Many questions." A spokesman for the Federalist Society questioned Darrow's credentials: "He didn't even graduate from a top-tier law school? Has he ever clerked for a federal judge?"

Darrow spoke with reporters after the press conference. Like his namesake Clarence Darrow, he is plainspoken, even blunt.

"My parents wanted me to be a lawyer," he said. "They figured with the last name Darrow, I'd have a pretty good start." He chuckled with the warmth of a man accustomed to mirth. "Of course, we're no relation. It was just dumb luck they named me Gerald," he said. "But once Gerry Spence's name went up in lights, well, I knew the law was for me."

Darrow graduated in the middle of his law school class at the Thomas Cooley Law School in Lansing, Michigan, and went on to become a personal injury lawyer in the Detroit firm of Michigan legend Geoffrey Fieger. His father worked on the assembly line at Chrysler before succumbing to a heart attack two years before Darrow was graduated from college. His mother worked as a clerk at Blue Cross and Blue Shield. He enjoyed early and spectacular success as a trial lawyer, winning multi-million dollar verdicts against the auto industry and insurance companies. But after ten years of civil work, he had an epiphany.

"There's only so much money necessary to keep a roof over your head. I woke up one morning and didn't like the man looking back at me in the mirror. So I sold the Audi and applied for a job as a public defender," he said. "I was also divorced from my wife. It still hurts to think about that and the pain I caused my kids." He eventually landed in New Britain, Connecticut,

in a community court serving an economically distressed community. "My bankruptcy helped knock the false pride out of me. I know human need and fear," he said.

Darrow remarried six years ago. His wife is a state police officer. "Passion makes strange bedfellows," he chuckled.

For the past seven years, Darrow has defended "more people than I can recall" in cases ranging from murder, child sexual abuse, drug sales and bank robbery to minor offenses such as promoting prostitution. "I'm more comfortable with folks like the ones I grew up with," he said. "I'd like to try my hand at white collar defense, but that work doesn't come to a public defender."

Darrow is an only child who graduated Detroit's Edwin Denby High School in 1986. He played football and worked part-time sweeping factory floors in high school before attending Eastern Michigan University in Ypsilanti, Michigan. "I really wanted to go to University of Michigan, but I didn't have the grades," he said. "I did pretty good in law school, though. And I love the courtroom."

An administration spokesman acknowledged that Darrow was an unconventional choice for the high court.

"The president had his pick from an extremely talented group of academics and appellate court judges," one source said on condition of anonymity. "But he promised change. He wanted a nominee who shared the same rough edges most Americans live with each and every day. As we were vetting candidates we came to the depressing realization that all these folks looked the same. The president wanted to leaven the Court with a person ordinary Americans would appreciate."

The Detroit Free Press once referred to Darrow as "brilliant and audacious" for his trial work on behalf of prisoners in the Wayne County jail. He is reported to have tried in excess of 150 cases to a verdict. He has argued scores of appeals in state and federal courts.

"The man knows his way around a courtroom," said Salmon Penderton, of the Connecticut Bar Association. "He is respected and admired by almost everyone in the criminal justice system. Sure, he's rubbed some folks the wrong way. But he's the guy they call when trouble comes."

Vermont Senator Patrick Leahy, co-chair of the Judiciary Committee, promised to give Darrow a fair hearing.

"We know nothing about the man, but I hear he is a capable lawyer. Perhaps that's all that is required. It could be refreshing to have a nominee unencumbered by commitments to legal interest groups." Leahy promised a prompt confirmation hearing.

Darrow seemed nonplussed by the furor with which his nomination was met.

"Sure, I want the job," he said. "But if it's not meant to be, it's not meant to be." He then removed his sports coat and entered the Butner Federal Medical Center, a federal prison, to visit a client committed there for the purpose of being restored to competency. "This is where the law lives," he said, as he entered the prison door. "I wonder if I can make what I see here a reality for the other justices."

Well, all right, the story never appeared anywhere other than on a web page I created as hoax. It is fiction. But it is my dream. We need a trial lawyer with experience defending people on the Supreme Court. That should not really be asking too much. There are nine seats, after all. What would be the harm in placing someone on the Court who knows what it is like to face the government as an adversary?

Those who expected boldness from President Barack Obama in his appointments to the Court have ample reason for disappointment. He said he wanted a lawyer with real world experience. Just how real was the president prepared to get? Both his appointments thus far, Sonia Sotomayor and Elena Kagan, have been cut from the same star-studded mold of Ivy League law graduates who served either as appellate judges or legal academics. These sorts of folks are typically clueless about what transpires in our nation's courts on a day-to-day basis. It is as though we have appointed a brilliant faculty to teach surgery without the teachers ever having actually laid hands on a living, breathing body. What is the president thinking?

Not long ago, I enjoyed dinner with none other than Charles Fried, a former solicitor general of the United States, and a long-time Harvard law professor. (He quipped that he had thrice been voted tenure, having moved in and out of the academy in the course of his career.)

Fried is everything I am not—he is witty, urbane, self-assured. It was hard not to feel envious of the man. While I cannot say he was born to the manor, he inhabits a rarefied world. My world is plenty more visceral and a whole lot less prestigious.

The two of us had been invited to participate in a discussion on appellate advocacy by Sonia Sotomayor, then presiding as an appellate court judge on the United States Court of Appeals for the Second Circuit. She taught a seminar at the Columbia law school. Shortly thereafter, she was appointed to the United States Supreme Court.

I get invited to do things like this from time to time, and it always surprises me. I am usually the entertainment section of a program. Let the serious speakers trot out their doctrinal statements and learned comments. Then I waltz in for comic relief: in Fried's and Sotomayor's presence, I felt that I was there perhaps to serve the refreshments. As the evening began, I was intimidated; the weight of the chip I carry on my shoulder oppressed. It was hard to shake off.

We ate at a quiet spot in Manhattan after class. It will remain memorable for as long as I practice law. There was a "pinch me" quality to the entire experience. Fried represented the United States before the Supreme Court; Sotomayor went on to become a justice. Me, I was due in court the next morning on a child sex case. It seemed dissonant. My one and only trip to the United States Supreme Court, on behalf of a prisoner beaten by guards, resulted in a 9-0 drubbing.

One comment Fried made in the course of the evening stuck with me. We were discussing the sorts of pressures a lawyer feels in a high-stakes case. I said something about my heart having been broken in one case or another. Fried did not miss a beat. "My heart has never been broken by a client," he said.

I was surprised by that remark. On reflection, I feel bad for Fried. The law is about human drama and private turning points made public. Heartbreak really is part of the law. I believe the professor said he'd never stepped foot in a courtroom until the age of 50.

Fried's argued some 26 or 27 cases before the Supreme Court. He argued *Daubert*, a case that remade the law on the use of expert testimony in our courts. And he has written wise and wonderful books on the law. But somehow I came away saddened. All the brilliance in the man but yet no blood left on the floor of his local court. I wonder whether that same sort of cerebral detachment typifies the Supreme Court bar, and the justices themselves. I suspect it is so: the law is worse for it.

The current court is composed entirely of former federal appeals court judges and legal academics. All but one got their professional tickets punched at two of the nation's premier status factories: Harvard and Yale. Three of the current justices have never even worked in private practices. As lawyers go, the current justices are glittering gems. It is an elite group, long since detached from the world the vast majority of folks inhabit.

When President Obama opposed John Roberts' appointment to the Supreme Court, he said "adherence to precedent and rules of construction will only get you through the 25th mile of the marathon." What concerns the president is the view during the last mile, a view that takes account of "the broader perspective on how the world works."

Has Obama forgotten his promise to appoint someone with real world experience? I wrote an open letter to the president on my blog, asking that. I received no answer.

"Mr. President, those who walk the corridors of power don't run marathons. A federal appellate court judge sprints. A state lawmaker runs hurdles. A trial judge is a middle distance runner. And former governors and chief executives of government agencies are, at best, specialists in the 10,000 meter run. The men and women who run the law's, and life's, marathons, are trial lawyers.

"A trial lawyer knows about raw human need and the law's rough edges. It is a trial lawyer's job to find the intersection of terror, fear and tears with the high doctrine and principles of the law. Not one member of the current court has ever sat with a client and his family during jury deliberations to discuss what will become of a family should the client be sent to prison. Not one of these legal scholars has ever told a person that the law's reach will not embrace the harm they have endured. I cannot fathom Justice Scalia counseling a client about sovereign immunity.

"And be careful, Mr. President. When I refer to a trial lawyer, I am not asking you to troll the big leagues. Don't call David Boies or the other so-called stars of the bar representing big clients with deep pockets. These lawyers are at best half-marathoners. They don't know what it is like to stand in the well of a court pleading for justice long after their client has run out of money to pay them.

"I am not a scholar of the Supreme Court, so I do not know the answer to this question: when is the last time a lawyer who made his living from fees earned representing ordinary working people sat on the Supreme Court?

"The bar's elite will shudder at the thought of an uncouth lawyer sitting atop justice's pyramid. But the shuddering really reflects the conceit of those who view the law as little more than a pyramid scheme. The law is not science. There is no Platonic elite governing by means of eternal truths exposed briefly to view in ordinary conflicts. The law is simple: it is civilized society's way of brokering peace in the face of conflicts rubbed raw by human need. A man dies, and another is accused of the killing; a mother cannot afford the rent for her home, and her landlord presses her; a child's parents do not provide the care a state official thinks necessary and now hearts are torn asunder. This is the world too many Americans inhabit. We do not command corporations, run large agencies, stride the corridors of power as lawmakers or judges. When we awaken in the morning, we hope, and the law is what we turn to when the hopes of conflicting parties threaten to turn into despair.

"Mr. President, you broke a mold when you were elected, or so it seemed. Hope flowed from the bosoms of millions who thought you would provoke change. Don't fall into the mold of offering the same old type of judge. Turn your back on Ivy walls. Tell the law's interest groups and their constipated doctrines of what the law is and should be to retire to their studies to inhale the choking smell of the wick. Leave the politicians and judges alone to enjoy their power. Pick a lawyer who is acquainted with sorrows and knows the grief of the real people in need who elected you."

Little did I know when I wrote this letter that I had recently had dinner with his first appointment to the Supreme Court, Sonia Sotomayor; he appointed her several weeks after I wrote my letter. Yes, her background as the child of a single mother living in a Bronx housing project gives her perspective. And "wise Latina" or not, she does diversify the Court. But by temperament and professional experience, she breaks no new ground. The same can be said of Obama's next appointee, Elena Kagan.

Only The New York Times could publish a piece of middle-class hagiography and expect readers to gush. I read the paper's glowing piece on then-Supreme Court nominee Elena Kagan's family with a sense of seething discontent: another child of privilege movin' on up. I wanted to throw away the complimentary silver spoon that came with that day's edition of the paper.

Ms. Kagan's father was a progressive lawyer and graduate of the Yale Law School. Her mother was a teacher at Hunter College High School. The couple worked together, played together, raised a family together. Ms. Kagan's brothers are accomplished and charismatic in their own right. The Kagan family piece in the Times felt like an episode of *Leave it to Beaver*; you know the episode, the one in which an Encyclopedia Britannica salesman drops off the new volumes and the family cancels their vacation to the Jersey shore so that they can sit home and read each and every volume, starting at A.

Sure, she is as intellectually capable as any of thousands of lawyers in the United States. She exudes the drab sort of conventional brilliance typical of a Mensa conference: whatever eccentricities she has are all of a predictable sort. The Times proved Tolstoy right: "Happy families are all alike..." So Elena Kagan sprang from the granola-like innocence of Manhattan's Upper West Side. Didn't Diane Keaton once express the sensibilities of this crowd with perfect pitch when, in a film directed by Woody Allen, she said: "Lah-De-Dah"? Simply put: the bed of privilege from which Kagan arose each morning interests far less than what she would do if she were required to pick up her bed and walk.

I am moved far more by the life story of Clarence Thomas, a child abandoned by his father, raised amid poverty and cared for by grandparents. Much though I dislike his jurisprudence, I can at least find something familiar in his biography. I suspect his life story resonates with more Americans than does that of Elena Kagan; so, too, the story of Sonia Sotomayor. Go ahead, call me a bigot, but haven't we had enough upper middle-class white people calling the shots?

Life's privileges rarely result in life-defining challenges. What is taken for granted is rarely noticed. I know this to be true from my wife's biography. Her mother became a Harvard professor, and the life my wife led shared many things in common with that of Justice Kagan. But what defined my wife was the shattering experience of seeing her father whisked off to federal prison for failing to take an oath of loyalty to the United States. She still recalls visits to a federal correctional center to see her father. She has a life-long sense of wonder about why a different vision of social justice is enough to make a man a criminal. I understand this secret sorrow of my wife's family; this sorrow is uniquely theirs.

If Elena Kagan struggled in her life, it was a struggle devoted solely to the main chance: hers is the master passion to succeed and bent to the exclusion of all else. She became a Justice simply because that is what she wanted from a young and tender age. Forgive me if I find this tale of ambition morally tedious.

The law is about broken dreams, passion recklessly spent, hope redeemed and the terror that comes of the confrontation of the irrational with the claims of reason. These struggles are lived daily in a place Justice Kagan has read about but rarely experienced, a courtroom. It chilled me to see another brilliant automaton take a seat on the Court. Justice Kagan is a fellow American and a fellow lawyer, but she lives in a privileged bubble. She could as easily be corporate counsel for a bank as dean of the Harvard Law School. She knows all the right and beautiful people. She is, sadly, a woman without discernible qualities other than a dogged determination to color within the lines.

Justice Kagan fit a mold that President Obama does not have the courage to break. How long before we have a trial lawyer on the Court, Mr. President? How long?

CHAPTER 17

HOW ABOUT A TRIAL LAWYER ON THE SUPREME COURT?

The next time a nominee to the United States Supreme Court makes his or her way to the Judiciary Committee of the United States Senate for approval, I have a suggestion: ask the nominee tough questions. If the Senators get gibberish in response, don't vote on the nomination. That would be a welcome change of pace. The Senate should withhold approval of a candidate if he or she believes it is inappropriate to comment on the issues that might come before them.

The confirmation process is, as Justice Kagan so aptly noted long ago, vapid. It is also a farce. The president nominates a candidate with whom he is comfortable, and then sends the candidate along to the Senate for confirmation. But the current manner of conducting these hearings transforms them into a meaningless beauty contest. Just how composed can a candidate remain while saying nothing at all?

Judged by the standards of the genre, Justice Kagan was certainly a success. She sat for several days before the Senate a stoic image, expressing little emotion as she was both praised and derided for her career as an ersatz lawyer. Forgive me my arrogance, but despite her brilliance, her law review articles, her professorships, her stint as dean at the Harvard Law School, her role as policy wonk in the Clinton

White House, and her brief tenure as Solicitor General, the woman is a stranger to the courtroom. I would not feel confident sending her to handle a misdemeanor charge on behalf of a client. Yet up, up, up she climbed the legal ladder. She climbed without her feet ever really touching ground. Every effort to get her to describe how she feels about such vital issues in our time as the reach of government power in the so-called war on terror, or whether all Americans, regardless of libidinal compass, should enjoy meaningful equal protection of the law, was met with the same vacuous stonewalling now typical of the hearings. It would be inappropriate to answer these questions, she says, because she might be called upon to decide them.

The wonder of it is that the Senate was complicit in this mealy-mouthed gibberish. Senators sat dumbstruck in something like awe, treating the candidate as though she were an oracle, a goddess who must be propitiated lest offense yield distant and divine scorn. Supreme Court justices are not high priests; rulings aren't oracles. Decisions by the Supreme Court are little more than judgments about how best to reconcile the competing imperatives reflected in the cases and controversies finding their way into the nation's courts. We look to the Supreme Court to settle the law in areas where pragmatic legal doctrines collide, where the past provides little guidance to what the future should hold.

It is not asking too much of a candidate for this lifetime seat on the nation's highest tribunal to tell us what commitments they bring to the Court. We are entitled to more than the empty promise to be fair and impartial. The current hearings are little more than pre-printed wedding vows. By mystifying the confirmation process with empty form, we trivialize the law and show scorn for the

American people. What message does the silly chatter send? That the law is deep, mysterious, its ways not capable of being charted, much less understood, by the ordinary people who must simply trust the wisdom of a justice and then obey her commands? That's silly. The law is merely applied principle. Legal doctrine, like Senatorial custom, changes. Is it too much to hope the next time around that the Senate's conception of its advice and consent will be transformed into something meatier?

When Kagan was nominated, I was crestfallen; another seat taken by a lawyer with no sense of what takes place in the trial court. I wrote the following open letter to Justice Kagan after she was confirmed:

"You did it. You set your sights on one of the nation's top jobs and spent a lifetime pursuing it. You spared no effort to accomplish your goal. You bent your will steadfastly and brilliantly to the task. Your resume glitters. You are a star of the bar, and now a Justice on the United States Supreme Court. Congratulations, Madame Justice. As you sit in your new chambers today, you should feel justifiable pride in all that you have accomplished, and you should look forward to the future. No one, least of all me, can take it away from you. You are a brilliant woman and now, finally, a jurist.

"But you have still never stood next to a man or woman in the well of a court who risked everything in a confrontation with the government on the result of a verdict. Sadly, not one of your colleagues has ever done that. You join a club of jurists who determines what the law is and is not, but yet lacks any critical perspective based on experience of the law's power to shatter the lives of little people. I hope you can understand, Madame Justice, why some of us view your ascension to the bench as simply more of the same old brilliant gruel.

"Our paths have never crossed, and there is a good chance they never will. I did not attend an Ivy League law school; I am not a law professor; I have never worked for the federal government or a big firm. I graduated from a second-tier law school, the University of Connecticut, and have spent the overwhelming majority of my career representing folks accused of crimes or suing state actors under federal civil rights statutes. I lack the diplomatic and social skills to garner the necessary support to become a judge. Most days, it is simply a struggle to pay my employees and meet my firm's expenses. My clients typically have little or nothing with which to meet the challenges of a prosecution.

"By the time a case of the sort I handle reaches you, the client is long forgotten. If there was an error at trial, the record speaks for itself. The man whose life depends on your ruling is someone you never see. It worries me that you have never once in your career sat with a client facing indictment and listened to him plead with you to make prosecutors understand that their perspective on the facts is wrong. It worries me that the errors you will dismiss as harmless aren't of the sort you have ever even seen committed in a courtroom. A jury is for you merely the stuff of legend: you've never asked a jury for anything. You think *jury* and you see a room of people presumed to be reasonable and presumed to follow the law. Madame Justice, there are no reasonable people; there are merely people with reasons. But how would you know that?

"Years ago, I argued many cases before a colleague of yours, Sonia Sotomayor, when she sat on the United States Court of Appeals for the Second Circuit. I found her always to be well prepared and possessed of a keen and penetrating intellect. She was one of the few judges on that panel who seemed actually to enjoy the intellectual give and take of the law. But time was always short at argument. She had a tendency to ask a hypothetical question and then press me to move on when I tried to answer it. One day I stopped her when she did that. 'Judge Sotomayor,' I said, 'you did that last time I was here. I'd love to engage you in a philosophical debate about these issues. When are you going to call to invite me to dinner for us to hash some of these issues out?'

"Imagine my surprise a year or so later when Judge Sotomayor called. This was before she was nominated to the Supreme Court. I will count as a high point of my career a dinner I had with her and former Solicitor General Charles Fried in Manhattan. Yes, I was overmatched intellectually, and lacked the sense to listen more: but for a moment, I felt that the law was the common possession of us all, and that three lawyers of differing perspectives and temperaments could share views and learn a little something. I give Justice Sotomayor credit for not forgetting that the law is not all glitter and polish: that she reached into the ranks of the bar to listen and to exchange views moved me. She has not forgotten where she came from, and although she worked as a prosecutor and not a criminal defense lawyer, she never forgot the sights and sounds of a trial court. Get to know Justice Sotomayor, Madame Justice. Whether Wise Latina or not, she has plenty to teach. And go ahead and tell her Norm sent you.

"There are no former public defenders on the Supreme Court. No trial lawyers. Every justice is a variation on the same theme: Ivy League, former federal law clerk, former judge or dean. Are people's lawyers not good enough for the high court? What message does that send the very people whose lives are often defined by the decisions the Court makes?

"Cherish your new role, Madame Justice, but please don't get too comfortable. Try to learn about trial, about the rights at issue in a courtroom. Never again will you look for work or need to aspire to anything other than excellence and the pursuit of justice. Go ahead and unpack your boxes, settle into the palatial chambers bought and paid for by the people. But try, please try, to remember that the decisions you make are about real people in crisis."

If you think that trial experience doesn't matter for a Supreme Court justice, I urge you to read Justice Sonia Sotomayor's dissent in *Skilling v. United States*. Having actually tried cases, albeit as a prosecutor, Sotomayor is not uncritically seduced by the embrace of a cold trial record. She knows better. Not many judges, or, for that matter, justices, do.

The *Skilling* decision has been the subject of a lot of commentary, but almost all of it is focused on the court's limitation of white collar prosecutions for theft of honest services. Prior to *Skilling*, almost any act of dishonesty or deceit by an employee, whether in government service or private employment, was enough to land you on the wrong side of federal crosshairs. After *Skilling*, at least on the surface, only conduct related to bribery or extortion will support such a prosecution: the Court held that to do otherwise would yield a statute so vague as to leave us all guessing as to what was and was not a crime; it would also empower prosecutors to pick and choose defendants almost at will, for reasons that often smell of politics. (I say only on the surface, because a group of senior lawyers in the Justice Department have formed a work group deciding how best to live in creative harmony with this rule. Expect more standardless prosecutions just this side of silly.)

But the honest services claim was only one part of *Skilling*. The former Enron executive also claimed that he had been deprived of a fair trial by the trial court's decision to deny his motion for a change of venue. Among other things, the panel of jurors was so saturated with hostility whipped up by the media, that sitting an impartial jury was impossible, he claimed. Try as it might, the trial court could not, and did not, seat a panel of jurors prepared to decide the case solely on the evidence presented in the courtroom.

Skilling's lawyers asked for lawyer-conducted voir dire as a means of flushing out bias and making a record in support of a change of venue. The trial judge denied the request, stating that in his experience jurors were more candid with judges than lawyers. Only a federal judge could buy this specious swill. The conduct of voir dire by federal judges is almost always a farce. Put an authority figure in a black robe on an elevated perch and set him loose on prospective panelists: most would-be jurors are so intimidated they'd agree to just about anything the judge suggests with his questions. This God-in-the-box form of voir dire is meaningless. Almost no one is prepared to challenge the mighty Jehovah when he sits wielding a gavel. Distrustful as folks may be of lawyers, they are at least more inclined to be honest with them.

I recall a case in Bridgeport, Connecticut years ago, in which a federal judge permitted lawyer-conducted voir dire. I was the last lawyer in a series of lawyers to speak. The panelists were tired and irritable by the time I was permitted to speak. One of them took a verbal swipe at me early in my questioning. The hostility spread like wildfire. Soon, several wiseacres were challenging me, suggesting my client would be better served by a better and different lawyer. I hung in there, thanking the folks for their honesty. I was afraid of that group, but treated them with respect. The respect was returned a week or so later when the jury acquitted my client of worker's compensation fraud charges. I would never have learned about the dark underside of that group so long as the judge chirped along, producing polite, almost grade-schoolish answers to his questions. Judge-conducted voir dire is, I repeat, a farce.

But few on the Supreme Court saw that in the *Skilling* case. The glittering intellects sitting on high buy what is printed on the page, and why shouldn't they, since that is all they ever see of a trial court? Writing for the majority, Justice Ginsburg cited the trial court's confidence in its ability to get candor from jurors as though it was an authoritative pronouncement. That is simply not credible, as any trial lawyer with more than one trial under his or her belt will tell you.

What's worse, the majority was so in love with the cold record in this case and so lacked critical perspective that it accepted the claim that jurors were not biased once they but uttered the pledge that they could be fair. Never mind the halting and confused comments leading to this profession of faith. All was forgiven once a juror declared she could believe.

Justice Sotomayor was not so easily fooled. I submit that is because she has been an advocate in a courtroom. She knows a thing or two about how jurors react when facing a judge determined to pick a jury as quickly as possible. (It took all of five hours to select the Skilling jury, this in a town ravaged by the Enron bankruptcy.)

Consider the following: jurors were selected who expressed reservations about whether they could be fair, and had intimations that Skilling might just be guilty before the evidence began. It wasn't enough for a juror to be disqualified as biased if they uttered "shame on him," of Skilling. One potential juror couldn't honestly say whether he could afford Skilling the presumption of innocence. That's okay, the trial judge ruled, so long as the juror could ultimately be persuaded to answer "yes" to a question about whether he would acquit if the government failed to prove guilt beyond a reasonable doubt. Sotomayor's dissection of the trial judge's voir dire is grim reading. It seems the trial judge was disposed to sit just about anyone with a pulse.

Justice Sotomayor, joined by Justices Stevens and Breyer, would have reversed Skilling's conviction because she thinks his panel was unfair either in appearance or in fact. I submit her dissent would never have been written if she had never seen with her own two eyes just what goes on in a courtroom. She knows that a record reflects words on a page, but that those words are but a reflection of a more nuanced reality. Her dissent is a sobering reminder that the quality of justice meted out by the high court is a reflection of the experience of the justices presiding. A court composed largely of jurists who have never been other than tourists in a courtroom is a court less credible than it ought to be.

Trial experience should be required before a judge takes the bench. Our trial courts, too, suffer as a result of an inept judiciary.

The next time you hear a judge whining about the vanishing trial, tell him or her to cut the crap and let the litigants get it on. Trials are vanishing because trial lawyers are being papered to death with meaningless bullshit. That's because most judges have about as much trial experience as a nun in a whore house: You can read all you want about what it's like to get screwed, but until you're flat on your back screaming "Jesus," all you know is what you've read. Nobody ever got pregnant reading pulp fiction.

Dahlia Lithwick of *Slate* argues that partisan gridlock has resulted in vacancies in 102 of 854 federal judgeships. This product of partisanship has created a non-partisan crisis in the courts. "Every day Americans look to the courts to address problems affecting their daily lives. With the high number of vacancies, their ability to stand up for their rights will be unacceptably delayed," Lithwick quotes Nan Aron at the Alliance for Justice as saying.

I've got news for Lithwick: fill the court with a bunch of paper-pushing bench jockeys, and ordinary Americans still aren't going to get justice. The courts don't function because they have succumbed to a managerial ethos. Rather than let cases go to trial, judges are papering lawyers to death. The reason Americans lack confidence in the courts is that most Americans can't get their cases heard in any meaningful way in court any longer. Judges are killing the jury trial.

The problem with the courts isn't a lack of judges; it is the sort of judges we get. There is a dearth of trial lawyers on the bench. What we end up with are transactional lawyers or so-called litigators—folks whose view of lawyering is confined to walking the desolate path of paper trails. Hence pre-trial management reports, damage analyses, interrogatories, requests for production, motions for more definite statements, motions to dismiss, motions for summary judgment, pre-trial memorandum, trial briefs: I suspect most federal judges wet themselves at the prospect of facing a jury because, truth be told, they have never faced a jury as a lawyer. Not one of these devices found their way into the Seventh Amendment's majestic promise of jury trials in civil cases. Why are we permitting federal judges to deprive us of a right others died to secure?

Connecticut has a full complement of Article III lifetime appointees to the bench, but still the docket creeps: dark courtrooms are unoccupied while keyboards click in chambers. Permitting juries to hear cases seems to be a dreadful prospect. An imperial judiciary doesn't want we the people anywhere near the administration of justice. The rare case that gets to a jury has run a gauntlet of judicial manipulation that leaves little for jurors to decide. And then, on the civil side, judges are free to hack away at damages or set aside a judgment they don't like. Popular distrust of the courts is not due to vacant judgeships; no, discontent with the courts arises from the kind of judges doling out justice.

Jury trials were once a crown jewel in the social life of small-town America. In the days before radio and television, folks flocked to courtrooms to watch the great dramas of the day unfold. Advocates bedeviled not just jurors but spectators with their rhetoric, and juries, speaking quite literally as the conscience of the community, were free to decide both questions of fact and law. A jury trial was something akin to a constitutional convention; great issues were placed before the community in a public forum.

Times have changed.

Explicit jury nullification has been abandoned in the federal courts and in the overwhelming majority of state courts. Television has made a mockery of the judicial process with cheap and easy entertainment taking the place of forensic contests. Those cases that get to trial are rarely reported any longer in an era of declining newspaper subscriptions: many papers economize by eliminating court reporting. And, worst of all, judges now seek to manage cases before they get to trial, eliminating most conflicts from the light of day and deciding cases based on mere passage of papers. Jurors, once the heart and soul of a community, are marginalized; judges are lionized. Juries are increasingly unnecessary.

If there is a crisis in the courts, it is not because there are too few judges. Rather, the crisis arises from the fact that few judges, even on the Supreme Court, have any real comprehension of what a trial is. Trials are vanishing, and so is public confidence in the courts. Putting a fresh batch of judges on the bench won't change a thing if those judges have the heart and soul of a backroom fixer. If we want public confidence in courts, we must restore trial to the role it once had as a public means of resolving conflicts. Let juries speak, and put the umpires back behind the plate, calling balls and strikes and leaving the game to those who know how to play it. Or, for those of you who insist on metaphorical consistency, send the virgins back to the convent: masturbation is not a spectator sport.

CHAPTER 18

A NOBEL PRIZE FOR WIKILEAKS?

The significance of the Protestant Reformation lays not so much in the proliferation of new, and non-Catholic, theologies: early Christianity was a wild cacophony of conflicting views of Jesus. It took centuries for orthodoxy to emerge. For more than a millennium this orthodoxy was maintained by use of censorship and institutional power. But the printing press changed all that. There could have been no reformation without the printing press. Access to the Bible in the vernacular made the competing versions of the truth possible. So if you worship in a Protestant church, say a prayer of thanks for Johannes Gutenberg, who developed movable type in 1440.

Martin Luther gets most of all the credit for kicking off the reformation. When he nailed his 95 Theses to the door at the church at Wittenberg in 1517, he sparked a revolution. Soon firebrands throughout Europe were demanding the right to interpret the Bible for themselves. These revolutionaries were armed with Bibles written not in Latin but in their national language. The very first Bible to be prepared on movable type was printed by Gutenberg in the 1450s.

I am reminded of Gutenberg, Luther and the power of ideas to change the world by Julian Assange and the reactions of the world's governments to WikiLeaks. Assange turned himself in to British authorities after Swedish authorities put a request to Interpol's 155 member nations to arrest him. Ostensibly, he is wanted for questioning by Swedish authorities over claims that he was a cad with a couple of jilted lovers. But these reasons are mere pretexts.

Assange became an international pariah because, like Luther, he spoke inconvenient truths to power. He exposed governments as liars, striking at the theology of deceit with theses accessible the world over. He used a technology even more powerful than the printing press; Assange and WikiLeaks used the Internet to tell truths governments would rather hide. For this, governments will seek to crucify him.

One government after another sought to shut down access to WikiLeaks so that these governments could control what is and is not capable of being known. Then big business got in on the act. Amazon, PayPal, and MasterCard all joined ranks to deprive Assange of access to the world's most movable type. Our government is now prosecuting those who protested the cowardice of the cash cows.

Our latter-day popes and cardinals want a world in which they control access to the truth. But I suspect that WikiLeaks's tactics are here to stay. Go ahead and crucify Assange, but the information reformation has begun.

About sixty years passed between the time the first Gutenberg Bible was printed and Luther's bold act of revolt. Things happen more quickly in our day and age. It has taken only several decades for the Internet to yield its Luther. Now that Everyman is a printer, there will be no stopping the free flow of ideas and information. Governments can try, but their efforts lack legitimacy. When democracies committed to transparency and businesses proclaiming the value of open markets seek darkness and a censor's restraint, it becomes obvious that the reality of power and the facade of rhetoric are on a collision course. Ideas can be suppressed by power, but not forever. "When a coin in the coffer rings, a soul to heaven springs," Sixteenth Century reformers quipped. They protested the Catholic Church's sale of indulgences, chits that could be turned in during the afterlife, as a means of making money. Luther turned a withering eye toward the practice. Where is that in my Bible? he all but thundered. New generations of men and women learned to read a book that Gutenberg brought them. They learned to interpret its signs and symbols for themselves.

Church and state are separate now. The Bible lacks the power it once had to form the entire sensibilities of a people. But we are still a people of texts, and we still live in the shadow of a government that makes a claim to legitimately use power, or authority. Our secular Bible is the rule of law. Democratic leaders worship at the church of transparency.

But now that Assange has nailed his own 95 Theses to each of our doors, how are we to forget, much less forgive, the lies our leaders tell us? If our governments are based on consent, where is it written that we have agreed to be led by liars and hypocrites?

"When a government by its spokesman speaks, suppression of the truth is what it seeks." That's a call for a new reformation. Where this one leads is every bit as open a question as was the remaking of Europe in the wake of the Reformation. The nation-state was but a fantasy when Luther first spoke. What shall replace today's parochial claims of sovereignty? Julian Assange was, in retrospect, an historic inevitability, despite his sometimes offensive personal idiosyncracies. The truth cannot be made the property of church or a government.

The prosecution of Assange was inevitable, too. Those who pretend to hold the keys to the kingdom of heaven rarely let go without a fight. So now the fight is on. Assange will be prosecuted and naked emperors will tell us they are cloaked in robes we have given them. But they know better; they know that WikiLeaks is less an organization than an inevitability. They know, finally, the words of an ancient prophet, who wandered the earth for a brief time before he, too, was crucified. His message was simple: the truth shall set you free. His message still resonates two thousand years later. Censors in suits and ties cannot kill it.

I say Assange is no criminal and WikiLeaks is no criminal enterprise: if they are, so much the worse for the law that declares them so. They are radicals, striking at the very roots of power. Why not a Nobel Prize for WikiLeaks?

The first Nobel Peace Prize was awarded jointly to two men in 1901: Henry Dunant, the founder of the Red Cross, and an international pacifist named Frédéric Passy. Both challenged the prevailing madness that would soon consume the hopes of the world during the first World War.

The Nobel committee ought to award the next prize to WikiLeaks. It would reward sunshine in government, and be a fitting acknowledgement of the Internet's capacity to change the world. It might also put the world's governments on notice that lies, even the boldest and biggest of lies, can purchase security for only so long. Wars and rumors of wars swirl the globe, and government cannot stop them. Indeed, under cloak of secrecy, sovereigns strut the globe like so many tyrants, killing in our name and then lying about what they have done. Entire generations are taught to hate because they are fed lies by governments that prosper by dividing and conquering.

WikiLeaks is a new but powerful presence in the world. It was founded in 2006, and first appeared online in January 2007. Although its founders have not been identified, it has been represented in the public by Julian Assange. It operates under the slogan: "We open governments."

That is a bold and perhaps futile aspiration. Government thrives on secrecy; it is the custodian and beneficiary of one of the grandest mysteries of humankind -- the transformation of naked power used by one person over another into authority. This piece of social alchemy is what distinguishes a hoodlum's carjacking from the police seizure of an automobile. Authority is power plus the badges, indicia and symbolism of what we call legitimacy. The trouble with this magic is that the magicians too often become transfixed by their own sorcery. Tyrants thrive on secrecy, and when the world's democracies tell us that we must trust them and obey them without being told the truth, these governments demonstrate a too-comfortable familiarity with tyranny. Look to the Middle East my friends; something is happening there. Is it truth catching fire in the minds of men?

Can government ever be truly transparent in purpose and in operation? Can we the people ever really be trusted to know what, in a republic, is done in our name? Governing in a democratic society takes place atop the volatile confrontation of the ideal of participatory democracy and the imperatives of power. Or, to put it more famously and elegantly: all power corrupts, and absolute power corrupts absolutely. Even in a society that aspires to be open, government hoards secrets its agents claim are too explosive for the world at large to know. A state seeks to seduce its people into believing that national security requires us to trust those in the know. We the people are not to be trusted; we must trust and obey, there is no other way. WikiLeaks exposes this as cant and hypocrisy.

Are we to tolerate government by misdirection, lie and deceit? Should we prosecute people for demanding that government live up to the public faith we profess? A good citizen must be a good hypocrite, we learn. But there are no good hypocrites. There are only folks more inclined than others to make peace with lies. The price the lie-keepers exact for their uneasy conscience is authority. They lie to us, they tell us, because it is necessary to do so. Their lies protect us. Do you smell the reek of the stable? Or do you crave the velvet glove of security?

WikiLeaks seeks to attack that logic at its source. The organization has published more than one million documents online since it was founded. Obama administration officials are spitting nails and threatening criminal prosecutions.

We would not know as much as we know about extralegal killings in Kenya but for WikiLeaks. The world's governments wanted that secret kept. Neither would we know near as much about what the United States has been up to in Afghanistan and in Iraq. Our government wanted those secrets kept from us. Trust and obey, the sovereign says.

Harold Hongju Koh, the State Department's top legal advisor, wrote to WikiLeaks, claiming to put it on notice that new disclosures of these diplomatic cables could disrupt the nation's war on terror, endanger lives, and undermine efforts to thwart nuclear non-proliferation. The disclosures are illegal, Koh intoned.

Perhaps they are, in which case the law is, as Dickens once noted, an ass. Or just maybe the cables will show the extent to which our government resorts routinely to lies and misdirection in the conduct of our affairs. Perhaps the truth is why we have so many enemies. Are we fooling the people of Yemen when its government tells its people that the bombs dropped on its territory against suspected Al Qaeda camps were Yemeni, and not American? A cable describing a meeting between General David H. Petraeus and Ali Abdullah Saleh reports Saleh's laughing that he just lied to his own Parliament by telling it Yemeni forces had been engaged in the bombing.

And whose interests are served by hiding the success the Chinese government has had since 2002 in hacking into the computer systems of the American government and those of Western allies?

The Nobel Peace Prize seeks to recognize the work of those who promote "fraternity between nations, the abolition or reduction of standing armies and... the holding and promotion of peace conferences." Publishing the world's secrets and putting them online for all to see takes power from the world's governments and gives it directly to the people. We can then confront those with a vested interest in standing armies and the badges and indicia of authority. This bold step may well promote peace.

Will it promote chaos? Sure. But who said chaos is bad? Only those folks pressing for order at all costs, and doing so with a gun held firmly in one hand. It is most likely a gun you paid for. And the person holding it is most likely a police officer or soldier living off the taxes you pay. What would be the harm in sharing information to stop hypocrites from killing in the name of justice?

WikiLeaks matters because government lies, and the United States government is no exception. Liars don't want the truth exposed, so they prosecute those with the courage to tell it. It really is that simple. Anyone who tries to tell you otherwise wants something the liars can confer, whether that be a job, access to power, or simply to be let alone to profit by playing the game of liar's poker known as good citizenship. But sometimes good men are not good citizens. When that happens, truth tellers are called criminals.

Julian Assange of WikiLeaks is a truth teller. He is accused of, *gasp!*, having sex without a condom. This is risible swill. When ordinary activities become a crime, the government gets to pick and choose whom to prosecute. Is it any mystery that the world's governments are on a manhunt for a man accused of having consensual, but unprotected, sex? This man, after all, publishes secrets the government tells us must be kept if we are to be safe.

These liars should feel shame, but they are incapable of shame so long as we give them our support. Instead of shame, we get self-righteous posturing by presidents, senators, prosecutors and all those with a stake in the game as it is played today.

An alumnus of Columbia's School of International and Public Affairs told the university's placement center to warn students seeking jobs with the federal government against reading documents posted on WikiLeaks websites. "The documents released during the past few months through WikiLeaks are still considered classified. [The alumnus] recommends that you DO NOT post links to these documents nor make comments on social media sites such as ... Twitter. Engaging in these activities would call into question your ability to deal with confidential information," the writer warned. Better to be the blind dupe of the plutocracy than a free and informed citizen of the world.

The governments of Russia, France, Thailand, China and the United States are seeking ways to block the free flow of information. Former United States Senator Joseph Lieberman, who hailed from my home state and can politely be described simply as a pig in a parlor, called upon Amazon to drop links from its site to WikiLeaks. The Internet broker obliged, prompting a backlash from customers offended that a purveyor of information would play cheap whore to Lieberman's pimpish request.

Information is like water, it flows without restriction unless blocked. When blocked, it can gather enough force to overcome a dam. The governments of the world now seek to obstruct the free flow of information with threats of prosecution, new laws, economic pressure and propaganda. They tell us all this is done so that leaders can perform vital affairs of state. Government needs freedom to lie, dissemble and to keep the people from knowing what is done in its own name.

But the printing press produced pamphlets, books and ideas that transformed the world, frustrating the censors' every effort to keep truth from flowing. The Internet, too, has the capacity to produce revolutionary change, perhaps helping to undermine the claims of parochial sovereigns everywhere. Of course, government will seek to strangle the truth and truth tellers.

A trusting people will tolerate this. But what happens when the people decide its government is unworthy of trust? Should we trust a government that bails out bankers and lets the homes of ordinary Americans be taken by foreclosure proceedings that rely on forged papers? Should we trust a government that sends our sons and daughters to die in conflicts picked on the basis of lies? (Ten years later, we're no longer looking for weapons of mass destruction; now we're just looking for a way out.) Should we trust a government that permits the rich to grow ever richer while ignoring the distress of the middle class?

No wonder the government lies. If it acknowledged the truth many Americans live, the walls would come tumbling down, and waters of rage would roil. Our government lies because the truth would expose it to be a naked emperor.

WikiLeaks matters because it shares inconvenient truths those we pay to represent us do not want us to know. Reporters Without Borders is calling upon all to support online freedom and the principle of "Net neutrality." It reminds us that the flow of information is a right worth fighting to preserve.

Julian Assange is a hero. So is WikiLeaks.

CHAPTER 19

NULLIFICATION NOW: SEX, DRUGS AND RACE

The most profound form of "stranger danger" apparent in the nation's criminal justice system arises not in the form of a sexual predator lurking in the shadows. No, the stranger who presents the gravest danger to our society is the lawmaker, judge or prosecutor who seeks to transform the criminal justice system into a blind assembly line. Only if we the people take back the power that is rightfully ours can justice be done.

I've refered elsewhere in this book to the Romeo and Juliet crimes, those offenses alleging that consensual sex can be crime when one of the participants is below a certain age. These laws are well-intended. But they can result in horrible miscarriages of justice. I was consulted not long ago about a case in the Southwest in which a young father was ordered to stay away from his own son. Why? The child had been conceived during an act of statutory rape. When even the child's mother objected to court-ordered fatherlessness for her child, the judge refused to listen. Can anyone truly respect a judiciary that produces such absurd decisions?

Many a young person is now in prison, a felon, a registrant as a sex offender or otherwise consigned to the indefinite purgatory known as sex offender treatment for the simple act of sexual curiosity. We put these young people on trial and never let the jury know what the consequences of a guilty verdict entail.

When these crimes are charged, a defendant is cast into the criminal justice system. And it is at this point that the newest form of stranger danger takes place. Jurors are often told only what must be proven by the state to find a defendant guilty. Jurors are given no, or, depending on the jurisdiction, little responsibility for punishment. We ask jurors to determine guilt in a vacuum, divorcing the crime from the consequences of being found guilty of it. This is moral cowardice.

The result is a system in which no one really accepts responsibility for what happens to a young person at trial. Lawmakers pass laws in their legislative sanctuary without any particular knowledge of the person on whose neck the law's yoke will fall. This one-size-fits-all approach often works injustice.

Judges then turn their back on justice when a defendant appears before them. If lawmakers mandate a mandatory minimum sentence, then a judge imposes it. The judge disclaims responsibility, taking the judicial version of the Nuremberg defense: he or she is, after all, just following orders.

Prosecutors, too, turn away from the consequences of their acts. Legislators create the crimes and penalties. Prosecutors just move the widgets down justice's conveyor belt.

In this way, government becomes unaccountable. When three branches of government—the legislature, the courts and the executive in the form of the prosecution—all turn their backs on one another, link arms, and dance a chaotic jig, the result is hardly a thing of beauty.

So where do defendants turn for justice? It used to be a jury was told it was free to serve as judge not just of the facts, that is, whether something occurred, but also of the law, to wit: whether the law was correctly applied. Almost every state now disapproves of jury nullification, as do the federal courts.

We need to revisit jury nullification. Folks involved in combating the excesses of the nation's failed war on drugs have done good work in focusing attention on jury nullification. Those in the reform community on sex offender laws need to forge a link with drug law reformers and spread the word about jury nullification. Let's teach juries about the consequences of what they do and of their right to refuse to be conscripted as assembly-line workers engaged in the detached work of finding so-called facts regardless of the consequences.

Here is a link you can use to learn more about nullification: www. jurorsforjustice.com. Is nullification unpatriotic? No. It's as American as apple pie. Don't forget for a moment that the greatest stranger danger lurking in the courts comes in the form of judges, lawmakers and prosecutors who don't want jurors to know the truth about what a jury is doing and why.

In the meantime, here is a radical proposal you can use if you are called to serve on a jury. You will be sworn to decide the case according to law. At the state's table a prosecutor will be seated, perhaps accompanied by an investigator. The prosecutor will call for you to hold the defendant accountable for his actions. But never forget for a moment the phantom in the room. The prosecutor claims to represent the state. But there is no state; the state is a legal fiction, remember? It is a fiction designed to serve the purpose of making life together possible, a governing authority of limited ends. Don't let the prosecutor strut and posture about holding the defendant accountable for his acts while all the while denying any accountability for what the prosecution is doing.

I am about to make a recommendation that has the power to transform the courtrooms of the nation into what they were always intended to be. Don't forget for a moment that in our Declaration of Independence we declared to the world that we were breaking from Britain to preserve and assert our right to a trial by jury as citizens. I am inviting you to take juries back, and to do so by the simple and elegant gesture of simply raising your hand.

Watch the panic when you do this. Raise your hand as the prosecution points an icy finger at the defendant, sitting next to his lawyer on the other side of the room. The prosecutor will panic. So will the judge. Odds are the arguments will cease for a moment. You might as a jury be asked to leave the room as the judge and lawyers convene out of your presence to decide what to do about this strange and miraculous event: a citizen with a question. Before you are asked to leave the room, stand and ask the following simple question: "What will happen if we return a verdict of guilty?"

You will be told that you are to decide simply the facts, out of context and without regard to the consequences. But in no other area of your life are you asked to make life-changing decisions without weighing the consequences. Tell the judge when he or she equivocates and evades this simplest of questions that unless you know what the consequences of your actions are, you cannot act. Remind the judge that the prosecutor is acting on behalf of the state, and that the state is a legal fiction. You as a juror have been selected as a representative of the state to see that justice is done. How can you do your job if you are denied the very accountability and responsibility the state seeks from the defendant? It cannot be done, I tell you. If jurors begin to insist that justice will be done, then justice will be done.

Consider the carnage in this the land of the free that comes of not letting jurors know the truth, and nothing but the truth, about what goes on in the criminal courts.

Did you know that the state of California imprisons more people than do the nations of France, Great Britain, Germany, Japan, Singapore and the Netherlands combined? We have 2.3 million people behind bars in this country. That is 25 percent of the total number of persons imprisoned worldwide. By contrast, the population of the United States constitutes five percent of the world's population.

There is something seriously wrong with these numbers. We call ourselves the land of the free, and then we imprison more people per capita than any other nation. Nowhere does the rhetoric and reality of American life collide quite so violently as it does in the criminal justice system.

I was thinking about that as I stood on line at the Department of Motor Vehicles to renew my expired car registration. Three white, middle-aged and prosperous looking folks were standing within earshot. The woman had just purchased a used Mercedes-Benz convertible. It was a dream to drive and ride in, she told the admiring listeners.

Talk then turned to how much she paid for it. It was a bargain, she reported: she paid $10,000. She wondered how much she would have to pay in taxes on the car, as she thought the car was more likely worth close to $20,000.

"For cars of that age, the DMV simply accepts your estimate of value," one man said. "You don't need to report the actual amount you paid and pay all that tax on the sale."

This struck the woman as a revelation. Her reaction surprised me. Here were three apparently prosperous Americans openly discussing tax fraud in a public place, conceivably within earshot of regulatory personnel manning the counters of the DMV. They assumed that cheating on taxes was all right, so long as you don't get caught, of course. In other words, there is nothing intrinsically wrong with tax fraud, so long as you can avoid the consequences: they found it morally acceptable to cheat but pragmatically undesirable to get caught cheating. These folks were would-be revolutionaries, demonstrating with their greedy chatter just how widespread a sense of illegitimacy has spread in our society.

A sense of legitimacy is the glue that holds a civil society together. Without legitimacy, a sense of fairness among free and equal people, there is really no meaningful social cooperation. Does the high incarceration rate in the United States reflect a legitimation crisis?

I think it may well. There are simply too many criminal laws. No one knows just how many criminal laws circumscribe the conduct of any of us at the state and federal levels. Prosecutors have broad discretion to charge or not on a bewildering range of offenses: I read recently that two lobstermen are now serving lengthy federal sentences for importing shellfish from Central America in plastic bags rather than boxes. We put people in prison for that?

Our penal code fails miserably when it comes to race, drugs and sex offenses. A young black man in the United States has a one-in-three chance of imprisonment during the course of his lifetime, as opposed to a six percent chance for a white male. We incarcerate folks sometimes for life for selling narcotics, but permit alcohol and nicotine to be pedaled without consequence. We make it a crime for young people to fall in love. For far too many Americans the criminal law is a foreign curse, a plague that falls upon them much like cancer and must be endured as a state-sanctioned illness. Over-criminalization breeds a crisis in legitimacy.

What is amazing is that we are doing this to ourselves. Rather than fighting back and asking questions, jurors far too often make decisions about people without demanding answers about what the consequences of their verdicts will be. We've gone mad, really. We incarcerate more and more Americans for more and more prohibited acts, and we don't even ask why. Perhaps that's why folks chat freely about cheating on their taxes in public places.

Books about race and criminal justice are typically depressing. In the war of the establishment versus angry black men, the establishment wins the power struggle, but is left defending a vulnerable castle. The moral high ground goes to the dispossessed. Because I am white by accident of birth, I am left banging a hollow drum.

Paul Butler's *Let's Get Free: A Hip-Hop Theory of Justice* is a welcome change of pace. Sure, Butler is an angry black man. He has plenty to be angry about. The lottery of life handed him a ticket that makes it almost impossible to win big, or to hold such winnings as he may acquire.

Butler was a federal prosecutor in Washington, D.C., in the public integrity division of the Justice Department. A graduate of Yale and the Harvard Law School, he was one day arrested and charged with simple assault. He went from the law's pinnacle to the bargain basement in which we sell black lives at a discount.

In truth, his experience as a criminal defendant was not all that jarring. But the experience radicalized him in a polite sort of way. He left government work, and became a law professor. His trajectory isn't exactly that of a modern rider on some underground railroad.

He retains the privileges conferred by attendance at a law school status factory. But, and this is the point, his heart is in the right place.

He believes in jury nullification and the role of jurors as a means of challenging the status quo. In a brief paragraph or two he asks what would happen in a world if decisions about social justice were made by those least advantaged in our society, a move perfected and made philosophically robust by John Rawls in his *A Theory of Justice*.

What group stands at the fringes of our institutions and power structure, looking in with hungry and angry eyes? Black men. And Hip Hop is the beat of this tribe. Can there be a Hip Hop theory of justice? That's a tall order, and Butler knows it. It is one thing to recite lyrics about the impact of mass incarceration of black men on those left behind, or about anger toward the police. These expressive moves reflect real tensions. Hip Hop hasn't yet found its Immanuel Kant yet; and it may never.

The system, to put it mildly, is a massive shell game in which judges refuse to accept responsibility for the sentences they impose, pointing to lawmakers who create mandatory minimums. But lawmakers are ignoramuses about what goes on in a courtroom: it's easy to chest thump in a legislative chamber and to pretend that one size fits all.

The criminal justice system lacks accountability, and we deprive the one body that could make a difference and speak truth to power of the information it needs to make reasoned judgments. I am referring, of course, to juries. Just how we have come to emasculate juries is a question Butler doesn't answer. He merely reminds how wrong the practice is. Read Butler, and then lend a hand in the struggle to set juries free to make morally responsible judgments.

Whatever else you do, ask questions if you are called to serve on a jury. It is your court. Take it back, if you dare.

CHAPTER 20

THE CHESHIRE HOME INVASION: KILLING THE AMERICAN DREAM

Truman Capote was alive and well in a Connecticut courtroom in 2010. At least he should have been. That's because the trial of Steven Hayes rivaled the horrible fascination Capote created in 1966 when *In Cold Blood* was published. His prose brought to the reading public the brutal murders in 1959 of Herbert Clutter, his wife and two of their children in Holcomb, Kansas. Capote's precise rendering of the crime and its causes was disturbing, yet beautiful in literary form. Terror striking at the heart of the American Dream sells: we love to hate the horrible. Witness box office sales at horror and slasher films.

But in July of 2007, terror became real in Cheshire, Connecticut. Two ex-convicts, Steven Hayes and Joshua Komisarjevsky, burst into the home of a popular physician in the dead of night in an affluent bedroom community. When they were done, Dr. William Petit Jr.'s wife and two daughters were dead. The killers sexually assaulted the mother and youngest daughter, an 11-year-old child, tying the children and their mother to their beds before setting the house afire and fleeing. Dr. Petit was beaten and left for dead; he managed to stumble out of the house, and into the hearts and minds of ordinary Americans.

All of the New England states except Connecticut and New Hampshire have abolished the death penalty as a barbarous anachronism. New York and New Jersey have also walked away from any claim that state killing is just. But Connecticut decided to seek the death penalty against the killers in the Cheshire cases. It did not do so on grounds of race: although the both the killers and victims were white, the crimes outraged. These murders took place in paradise. The world turned out to watch the first of the two trials, the case against Steven Hayes. Connecticut sought to kill to keep paradise secure.

Retired Supreme Court Justice John Paul Stevens was right to note that the death penalty is more often than not used against people of color. But he missed the larger point about the death penalty. It is not a measured tool of justice; it is a tool of hatred. We use it more often than not against people of color simply because the matter of race is far from settled in our society. The color line still separates and divides. Race-based hatred may not be a polite and politically correct sentiment, but it thrives in dark alleys and private rooms.

We hate the other, the thing that is different and threatens us. That hatred can take forms other than race-based rage. In the Cheshire case, it took an almost mythic form. When Steven Hayes and Joshua Komisarjevsky stormed the Petit home, it was as if they declared war on the American dream. A doctor's home, tucked in an idyllic suburban paradise: if such a location is not the safe object of our hopes and dreams, then what have we to unite us? There was a clamoring for death in my otherwise peaceful state unlike anything I had ever seen. It felt as though the entire world turned out to watch the trial. We gloried in every horrible detail of the trial, and then declared that the man must die. We made a hero of Dr. William Petit, a man who could not wait until the trial of Mr. Komisarjevsky before agreeing to appear on the Oprah Winfrey show, where he could be feted as the man we most want to pity. What spiritual vacuum produced this farce?

I was in the New Haven Superior Court the day the trial against Steven Hayes began. My clients were ordinary folks enmeshed in the ordinary sorts of chaos that are typical of a criminal defense lawyer's day: a woman cut her lover with a knife as they fought. The state claimed assault; we claimed self-defense. A mother and father locked a teenage daughter out of their house after beating her with a belt: if she wanted to behave like a street walker, then let her walk the streets and learn the many sorrows of a pimp's girl, they reasoned in a frightened rage. The state claimed assault and risk of injury to this child; we acknowledged a line was crossed but saw no point in sending these parents to prison as felons. Did I mention that my clients were all African-Americans?

Lines were drawn. A woman can defend herself against a man enraged, even by cutting him and sending him to the hospital, or so we claimed. A judge and prosecutor mulled whether to send caring parents who went too far to prison. Lines were drawn in these cases in a rundown courthouse on Elm Street across from the town green.

Around the corner, a different sort of line was forming at a different courthouse. This one was composed of reporters and gawkers, all of whom were gathering for the start of the trial of Steven Hayes, the murderer of a physician's family in paradise. This case has become the stuff of legend; it is national news. It was the opening day of trial. Crowds gathered, reporters gawked and even Twittered, sending electronic messages to the world at large as witnesses testified, the largest courtroom in the city was spruced up for the proceeding. A separate courtroom was set aside as a gathering point for supporters of the victims' family. It appeared as if there were even additional street vendors in the area, hoping to feed the masses worshipping in this macabre house of grief. Do I dare remind that the victims in this case are upper middle-class white folks?

The Cheshire case has been the quiet talk of judges and lawyers throughout Connecticut since the murders took place in the summer of 2007. I have yet to speak to a lawyer or judge who does not acknowledge, privately, that class matters in this case. One jurist shook her head just before trial started in something like sorrow as we talked about the blood red carpet being rolled out for the Hayes case. Had the victims been black and poor, residing in a housing project rather than a bedroom community, there would not be television trucks outside the courtroom and sketch artists watching the trial. There would have been no special coat of paint to patch over rough spots in the courtroom. There would be no death penalty sought.

Judges know this to be true, but are afraid to admit it. Lawyers know it to be true, but see little premium saying it: why there are paying clients in Cheshire, the hometown of the victims. Why offend Mr. Green's keepers? (Mr. Green, I should tell you, is the most hoped for of all telephone calls for a lawyer – a client with a fee.)

We want to say that justice is blind; blind to class, blind to color. But we all know better. The Hayes case proves it. Even the state's forensic laboratory was in lockdown: I was set to try a murder case in Hartford, a city about 45 minutes drive north of New Haven as the Hayes trial began. My client was white; the victim Hispanic. These are people of modest means. We were informed that the state's DNA analyst might not be available. The staff was "on call" for the Hayes trial. This abysmal business of seeking to kill Hayes created a caste system in the state's criminal justice system. It is a bizarre but unspoken truth behind closed doors: The New Haven cases get special treatment. Those of our privileged class and station were felled.

The trial began without fanfare. Three jurors decided for one reason or another that they could not participate in the case. One, an African-American, was interviewed on television. She thought, on reflection, the case would be too disturbing, too violent. Perhaps that is the truth. But she had been questioned at length about this in jury selection. Perhaps this woman of color just felt uncomfortable around a white lynch mob bent on killing.

Defense counsel conceded in his opening statement that Hayes had killed the children's mother. This simple burglary wasn't supposed to turn violent. But it did. The defense did not waste time on distracting cross-examinations as the trial opened. The state examined five witnesses in rapid succession, setting the scene for testimony the prosecution promised would be deeply disturbing.

I know all of the lawyers involved in this case; two of them, State's Attorney Michael Dearington and defense counsel Thomas Ullmann, are family friends. But this trial strained relationships. I regard Tommy as a hero: a lawyer's lawyer standing proud and unbent in the face of rage and passion to defend a friendless man. Tommy is a public defender, but, should I ever need counsel, I would beg him to take my case. He approached this case with a sense of grim necessity. It was a hard, impossible case: the fight is to keep the state from killing his client. It was a fight to the death. Daniel had been thrown into the lion's den.

Mike played the role of reluctant white knight. He almost apologized to the jury about the horror they would experience in the trial. But the tone seemed all wrong. There was no necessity for this trial. Hayes offered to plead guilty. Life without possibility of parole is not enough for the prosecution. It wanted another corpse, another horror. I look at Mike and I sense something like the abandonment of reason. Why do you, too, insist on becoming a killer, Mike? What will you do with the eye you pluck from Mr. Hayes' cold skull in retribution for the eyes he has taken? Will you pickle it, place it in a jar on some hideous shelf in the chaos of your office? There was no need for this blood sport. This death work is a choice Mike has made; that he now asks others to become as Hayes, self-conscious and deliberate killers, is a mockery of the reasoned and measured pose that justice requires.

This trial was a two act play. The first part, the guilt phase, moved quickly. The state bathed the courtroom in blood and horror, and then stood by in mock solicitude as the jurors wept. Mock solicitude, I say, because it was the state that insisted that this upper middle-class show trial take place. Hayes would long ago have begun serving his life without possibility of parole term if the state had let him. Under Connecticut law, Hayes was required to fight for his life. The real fight took place at the penalty phase, where jurors were asked not to compound the evil done to the victims with the evil of making killers of us all.

When people of color stumble and fall, the system grinds out a dismal sort of tune: but kill white folks in paradise? In that case, we invite an orchestra to the courthouse. Why this show trial, Mike? Why press ordinary jurors to the point of becoming killers? This is not justice. This is a costly psychodrama that demeans us all.

Trial was well-attended theater. Reporters lined up four and five hours before the gavel fell to get one of the 160 seats in the courtroom. There was gore aplenty for all.

CHAPTER 21

THE JOY OF SOCIOPATHY – THE CHESHIRE CAT SMILES

I wish I knew why motorists stopped to gawk at every bit of roadside carnage. We are drawn almost against our will to stare at the sorrow of others. I suspect the same impulse was at work in the trial of Steven Hayes. We could not get enough of the horror of it all. It was a slasher film made real. "More," we demanded, even as we decried the crimes as intolerable. We're twisted all right.

So is Joshua Komisarjevsky.

When Hayes' lawyers unveiled the prison diaries of Komisarjesky in an effort to save their client's life by somehow claiming the slaughter was not Mr. Hayes' idea, they did us a favor. We were invited to drink our fill of the fury that produced the Cheshire slaughter. No need any longer to guess what could transform Hayes and Komisarjevsky into killers: we read all about it.

"I'm not insane," Komisarjesky told us, "because I've seen whats (sic) in my head play itself outin (sic) reality. I've tasted, seen and felt that this pain exists externally." Later he wrote: "I was suddenly acutely aware of a seething cauldron of disconnected rage lying behind my sorrow; Repression's shaddow.... a reminder that all humans can be as inhuman as the animal species we are." (The misspellings are Komisarjevsky's.)

This killer writes easily of the great hatred within him. "HATE, just a word I carved into my left arm as a child," perhaps after his rape at the hands of another at age six. This hatred and rage went somewhere deep in Komisarjevsky, and lay in wait. He found a sick and twisted sense of power in his late-night escapades as a cat burglar, always robbing us not just of goods, but of the peaceful serenity we associate with home. His hatred festered, an aggressive instinct stoked to white-hot fury not just by the normal inhibitions of society, but by the utter impotence arising from his inability ever to recover what was taken from him as a child.

Komisarjevsky nursed his private rage, hardly able to accept its defining force; until that night in Cheshire, when he just let go. That was the night he saw his own terror in the eyes of others and realized he was real; he was no longer alone. He created soul mates. Some he destroyed; at least one, Dr. William Petit, Jr., he sentenced to the very prison he inhabited: a world of dark taboos violated, a world of mocking disdain for the restraints of civilization, a world where the desire to kill surfaced and could not be tamped down.

"Do you have the strength to speak the words that will condemn me to death for the things you see in yourselves? " he wrote. Is he talking to his potential jurors, or to all of us? For a lifetime he wanted to kill, and then he did, shattering every taboo we recognize as defining a civilized person. Now we too are invited to transgress. We, too, are asked to kill. Komisarjevsky whispers to the jurors: "Do as I did, you'll enjoy it."

I read Komisarjevsky's words and I wondered, really, about rubbernecking at highway accidents; I wondered about the breathless Twitter accounts by reporters attending the trial daily, all professing horror but seemingly so energized by this ringside seat at the gates of hell. If this were really something so strange, so horrifying that we could not bear it, we would not be hanging on every gory word. Are we insatiable because of some unconscious realization that we're all on trial, our secret rages laid out in a forum now for all to see?

I reread Sigmund Freud's *Civilization and Its Discontents*, trying to shake the sense of fatal attraction this case yields. I was reminded that our instinct for aggression is ever present and must be tamped down to do the work required to live together. Before we swore allegiance to the flag, we raged in our infantile need for instant gratification; all that opposed our will, our desire, our want, was foreign, a force first hated, then reckoned with, and finally held at arm's length in the uneasy truce we call culture and civilization. We never truly stop raging at reality's uncompromising limits: we are such stuff as frustration is made of. So we let off steam with dark humor, vicious wit, gossip, the thousand and one ways that we feed morsels to the beast within, the devil that never really dies, but lays in wait within every breast.

Until that devil breaks through the inhibitions we call civilization in the form of the impulsive acts of men like Joshua Komisarjevsky and Steven Hayes. They broke the toe-hold conscience chipped in the dark facade of fury, so we stare, each of us, knowing that what they did was wrong, and fearing that should their acts not be the work of isolated madmen, but of Everyman acting out of a shared secret rage we have tempered with the work of centuries, all would be lost. We stare at these men with an unstated and perhaps unconscious shock of recognition.

We all deny that we could ever commit such acts, spawned as they are from hatred and rage for the things we say we cherish. But we keep staring at what we say we hate. We can't help it, because at some level nothing human is truly foreign to any of us. We are all capable of the unspeakable, so we take solace in speaking about it, a shared sort of communal reinforcement of conscience's contested sovereignty. We recognize something dark, Komisarjevsky calls it his "shaddow", in this horror, in his acts of brutality. Most of us shudder at the recognition, but some are attracted to it. I am told that at least one woman from Alabama seeks to write to Komisarjevsky, sensing a soul mate or some lost soul to love. The men we confine to death row, and those we seek to send there, attract such odd love letters.

I am not excusing Joshua Komisarjevsky or Steven Hayes. They should be removed from society. Something in these men snapped and we cannot tolerate their acts.

But I worry that the public display of rage this trial yields actually loosens the inhibitions against savagery. Did Komisarjevsky let hatred and rage grow into an overpowering force as a result of his childhood rape? Perhaps. But what now of the rage of Dr. William Petit, Jr? What now of our rage? What occurred in Cheshire in the summer of 2007 is an outrage; it is beyond the bounds of what can be tolerated in a civilized society. We cannot live together if we do not stifle the aggression within that can so easily be mobilized into this lethal madness.

But the clamoring after these men's deaths represents a triumph of the very darkness we should be taming in the name of civilization. We do not civilize by killing; that is the act of savages living without the restraint of law. To overcome the artificial repugnance against killing that we call civilization is no easy thing. We must stir the very beast that Komisarjevsky let loose. We must become the devil we seek to slay.

We are transfixed by the Hayes and Komisarjevsky cases for dark and disturbing reasons. Their killing frenzy is a reminder of what we all know to be a simple truth: the devil lurks within us all. So we watch, and we cry for their blood in a court of law, hoping and pretending all the while that if we can kill in just the right way we can avoid becoming just like the men we love to hate. This is a dark trial not just because of what was done to a mother and her daughters. It is a dark trial because it reflects on the darkness within us all.

And so it happened after weeks of gore obsessively reported on for the world: a jury found Mr. Hayes guilty. The same jury then voted to have the man killed. It surprised no one.

A rump jury of twelve Connecticut residents carefully screened to exclude any member who opposed the death penalty voted to kill Steven Hayes. The state went a perfect six for six, winning each and every capital felony count. To those of us who oppose the death penalty, the verdict was a sheer act of barbarism. The state, which cannot give life, received permission to take what it cannot give.

In the end, there was but one hero in this case: the lawyer for Hayes, Tommy Ullmann. When an angry state lined up and volunteered to kill Hayes, Ullmann stood by his side. He walked his client to the rail of the jury box during closing arguments for jurors to behold the man. I thought in that moment that the spark of human decency would have been kindled and jurors would not kill. I admire the vigor and integrity of Ullmann's defense of his client. Ullmann sought something more than the common denominator of easy fear and rage. That this jury aimed so low is not Ullmann's fault.

But even Ullmann stumbled away from this new killing field talking nonsense. He told the press afterward that his client was actually happy with the verdict. He wants to die; the state will now do this for him. These words are as macabre as the penalty itself. In the end, the state and defendant stand staring at one another across a vast divide: both want death, apparently; but there will be a struggle to see who gets the sick privilege of imposing it. If, as supporters of this verdict contend, this case were about justice and not revenge, we'd stand silently by as Hayes took his own life, something he has already attempted to do while awaiting trial. But that won't do. We want the satisfaction of watching him die. We are all savages today, better than Hayes on his killing spree, but now of a similar kind.

After the verdict was taken, cameras were trained on the family of the slaughtered victims, microphones were thrust into the face of a man no one would trust to be on this jury, but from whom too many were willing to seek guidance about what was required in this case. We've made a cult of victimhood, and this victim became the high priest of rites that tap something primeval. Dr. Petit told the press this verdict was not revenge, it was justice. Does anyone really believe it is that simple?

Many states in the United States eschew the death penalty. So does every other democratic nation. We alone kill and call it justice. Other nations with civilizations and cultures far older than our own live just fine without worshipping the executioner's needle. Justice does not require killing. Justice does not require feeding flesh to the behemoth we call the state. Justice is not killing, ever. How proud now the strut of the prosecution, men who have persuaded jurors to do the unthinkable.

Consider now the moral posture of this case: Hayes has tried to kill himself, but the state stepped in to save him. Why? There is a presumption in the law against the rationality of suicide. A person cannot take his own life. So we stop him, and restrain him against his will. But for what purpose in this case? Did we save him so that we can accomplish the very goal he cannot have for himself? How much less satisfying his killing will be if he beats us to the needle. We feel cheated of the full measure of our desire for vengeance if Hayes cannot be dragged, full of regret and resistance, to the executioner's chamber. The hiss of the poisonous pumps that will deliver toxins to him will sound less satisfying if the words that precede them are "come, sweet death." We want Hayes to experience horror because we are his soul mates.

I fully sympathize with Dr. Petit and those close to the family who want Hayes dead. I too would want the destruction of those who harmed my loved ones. But this business of being hoodwinked into completing a private act of vengeance in the name of justice sickens. Yes, if there is to be a death penalty, this is the case in which to have it. But who said death was necessary or just? Those voices were kept off the jury. This was a death-qualified jury.

Ironically, even now Hayes will not be permitted to go silently into the night. Expect post-conviction hearings and appeals. Strangers will decide for him the timing of his death. He will sit now in a cell on suicide watch. The jury has sentenced him to die six times, but he cannot accept that verdict and agree to die. We must kill him against his will to enjoy the spectacle. So let's torture him, shall we, by keeping him alive for a decade or more as appeals run their course. This is spiteful sickness.

The crimes of Steven Hayes were sick and horrifying. So are the verdicts. And so, finally, are we.

It will be many years before a record is fully assembled about what role the media played in creating a death-chamber in the New Haven courtroom that was home to the trial. This was a verdict Twitter helped create.

The hero of this morality play was Dr. William Petit, Jr. His every move was studied and reported upon, as though he were something other than a man of sorrows, acquainted with unspeakable grief. Did he place his hand to his brow, or sigh, as the testimony was presented? On your mark, get set, type! was the silent imperative of the scores of press in the courtroom. And in unison, fingers pecked across tiny keyboards, each reporter trying to toss 140 characters into the electronic void first; each trying to show just how sensitive they could be about the sorrow and the horror, oh, the sweet horror, of it all.

This trial was transformed into a silly farce. On the one side, pure goodness, in the form of an upper middle-class white male, a physician no less, from a place called Cheshire. His was the sort of life we tell our children to seek. Work hard. Play by the rules. Get ahead. Until in the dark of night Evil comes a calling. Two hapless ex-convicts stormed into paradise. They raped and killed the doctor's wife, and murdered his two daughters, too. The doctor managed, miraculously and perhaps to his everlasting torment, to survive. His survivor's guilt is now buried beneath a call for justice.

The mother of a slain black man wandered the streets outside the New Haven courtroom as the Hayes trial took place. "My son matters, too," she told tired newsmen. You see, another trial was taking place in the building. This trial involved the killing of a black boy in the backwater of a distressed urban neighborhood. No one cared about this death. Only white deaths must be avenged in public spectacle.

Lawyers for Hayes have moved for a new trial, claiming that the courtroom was transformed into something other than a place of justice during trial. When dozens of reporters stare at Dr. Petit and report his every move, does that not infect the character of the proceedings? We all know it does, we just can't say quite how. Look at the techies staring frantically and zombie-like into their handheld devices at some coffee shop. They inhabit the twilight of the living dead.

The cold record in this case will not reflect this two-dimensional world. And those who know Judge John C. Blue, who presided over the trial, would not expect him to detect such a thing. He is a border collie of a jurist. Point him in the right direction, and he moves, cheerfully and with the alacrity of a teacher's pet toward his goal.

Claims about what went down in that courtroom will be perfected at a habeas corpus proceeding years from now. Social psychologists will testify about the power of silent cues, about something called sociometry and how a courtroom was transformed into a shrine. Whether Hayes will get a new trial then is doubtful. Too many people want him dead. You see, he is not just a killer. Hayes killed upper middle-class white folks. He killed the American Dream. That is simply unforgiveable.

And to think, we get to do this all over again in the trial of Joshua Komisarjevsky. I can almost see the lines forming all over again. We can't get enough of this gore. Justice Stevens is right. The death penalty is sheer barbarism, and we, barbarians all, love every twisted minute of such trials.

CONCLUSION

We get the government we deserve because we *are* the government. Not all of us can serve in office. Few of us have the wealth to stand down from our regular jobs. Not all of us can be lawyers, and a good thing, too. Very few of us can become judges. But all of us have the right and responsibility to serve as jurors. We all have the right to sit in a courtroom and serve as quality control for the justice done in our name. If you are unwilling to serve as a juror, then don't complain about what juries do; if you are unwilling to go and sit in a courtroom, in the spectators' gallery, to watch the sad machinery of justice grind up the poor and different, then don't complain about the law as unfair. If you are unwilling to stand up for the rights of another person who is hated and scorned because accused, then do not expect someone to assist you when you find yourself friendless, sitting on the wrong side of a courtroom next to a lawyer who may not be fully trained to help. I believe the courts present one of the most exciting opportunities for ordinary Americans to make a real impact on those who wield power. But to have that impact you must participate. Protest is not a spectator sport. A courtroom can and should be a revolutionary place.

Sadly, each of us, for less reason than you might think, stand on the threshold of prosecution. When everything is a crime, who can place their head on their pillow at night secure in the knowledge that they are free?

Why is the murder rate in the United States higher than that of any of the other 29 high-income member nations of the Organization for Economic Cooperation and Development (OECD)? We have slightly more than five murders per 100,000 population; the next nation in the list is Finland with less than half our rate. Just behind Finland are Israel, South Korea and Scotland. The place least likely to get you whacked? Iceland, followed closely by Japan, Austria, and, paradoxically, Finland's near neighbor, Norway.

Certainly the threat of prison and lengthy prison sentences do not serve as a deterrent. The United States incarcerates a higher percentage of its population than any other nation. And our prison sentences are obscenely long. In the past 25 years, our prison population has grown by 400 percent. Living in the land of the free, it turns out, is dangerous, and it is comparatively easy to lose the very freedom about which we boast.

According to researchers at Iowa State University, a murder costs the United States $17.25 million; a rape costs $448,532; and a robbery costs $335,733. Among the factors contributing to the cost of each crime are the costs of incarceration, the collateral costs of caring for the families of those incarcerated, the costs borne by victims in terms of lost opportunity. The study also factored in such costs as insurance and security devices. I am sure that other researchers will find fault with parts of the Iowa study's methodology, but the fact remains: crime is costly.

I am not suggesting that we should decriminalize violence as a means of reducing the social cost of crime: many of the economic consequences of crime would remain the same even if we were to decide not to punish serious crimes. But what I am suggesting is that our rage and our get-tough-on-crime attitude comes at a cost. The cost of all homicides in the United States in 2007 exceeded what was spent on the Departments of Education, Justice, Housing and Urban Development, Health and Human Services, Labor and Homeland Security in 2010. Instead of building a better country, we're throwing money away at a problem we are not solving.

This is especially so in death penalty cases. We are one of the few industrialized nations in the world to believe it is just to kill a person who has committed a crime. Yet the cost of such litigation far exceeds the expense of locking the same prisoner away for the rest of his natural life.

Our rage over crime and our rage to kill are costly, and ineffective, luxuries. We'd be wise to rethink the cost of hatred. Our prison population continues to swell, and our murder rate leads the world. We spend a fortune on prisons and not enough on schools. We've arrived at a Manichean sort of equilibrium, easily separating folks into categories labeled good and evil, but spending little time and resources deciding why in this, the land of the free and home of the brave, we cannot provide the material conditions for a decent life to a broad class of Americans.

We are the murder and prison capital of the world, and still people clamor to come to this country, so we enact harsh new laws to keep them out. I watch this and I can't help but think that evolution is a cruel mistress. We're just clumsy at adapting to the pressures evident and obvious in the world around us. Chaos? It's as American as apple pie! I love chaos; it's the law that scares me. It should scare you too.

AFTERWORD

Norm and I walked together on the wild side of the law for more than a dozen years. He has gone on to have a brilliant legal career. His genius in a courtroom is rightly legendary. The first time I actually watched him try a jury case I decided that I want to be him if I ever grow up. He is a magician with juries. And, like most magicians, he has a talent that can't be copied. He just does it and we lesser beings can only wonder how.

Now he has written a book. I expect it will become a sort of bible for aspiring lawyers, and probably for a lot of us old codgers as well. How he finds the time to do as much as he does is another of the mysteries about the man. He's constantly trying some case somewhere or other, at the same time running his antiquarian book store and managing the small farm where he lives and writing columns, giving lectures, you name it. And, as best I can tell, he is having fun. Lucky him, and lucky us who know him. Most lucky of all are the clients he serves.

John R. Williams
New Haven, Connecticut

ABOUT AUTHOR
NORM PATIS

Norm Pattis is one of America's leading trial lawyers as a veteran of more than 100 jury trials, many resulting in acquittals for people charged with serious crimes, multi-million dollar civil rights and discrimination verdicts, and successful criminal appeals. The Hartford Courant describes his work as "Brilliant" and "Audacious" while iconic attorney F. Lee Bailey describes him as "One of the Giants of  the Profession" and "Part of a Dying Breed of Slash and Burn Trial Lawyers."

Norm founded and leads the Connecticut-based Pattis Law Firm. He associates as trial counsel by attorneys across the United States for high stakes cases. His work has included defending capital murder cases, white collar crimes, sex offenses, drug crimes, misconduct by lawyers, doctors, and government officials, and other serious felony charges. He worked with Gerry Spence, who describes Norm as "One of the Best", at Spence's Trial Lawyers College in Wyoming, and as a faculty member for the National Institute for Trial Advocacy.

A frequent expert legal commentator for national media outlets, Norm Pattis is a popular speaker, syndicated blogger, and relentless advocate for people who face powerful foes. He lives in Connecticut with his wife Judy and owns a rural bookstore that has been operating since the 1890s.

To learn more about Norm Pattis visit:

www.normpattis.com

www.pattislawfirm.com

www.pattisblog.com

Norm Pattis is available for select speaking engagements. For bookings inquire through his representatives at Platform Strategy 360.521.0437

www.platformstrategy.com